Editor
Wanda Kelly

Managing Editor
Ina Massler Levin, M.A.

Editor-in-Chief
Sharon Coan, M.S. Ed.

Art Director
CJae Froshay

Art Coordinator
Denice Adorno

Cover Design
Lesley Palmer

Imaging
Rosa C. See

Production Manager
Phil Garcia

Publisher
Mary D. Smith, M.S. Ed.

Blake Staff

Editor
Sharon Dalgleish

Designed and typeset by
The Modern Art Production Group

Printed by
Australian Print Group

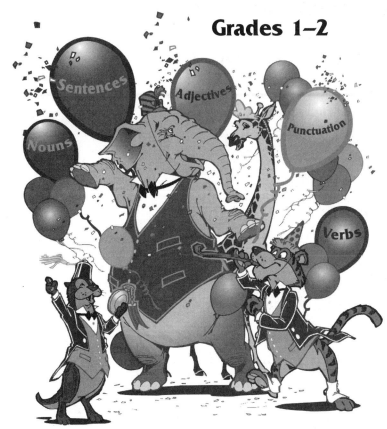

Grammar
PRACTICE

Grades 1–2

Author

Peter Clutterbuck

This edition published by
Teacher Created Resources, Inc.
6421 Industry Way
Westminster, CA 92683
www.teachercreated.com

ISBN: 978-0-7439-3620-0

©2002 Teacher Created Resources, Inc.
Reprinted, 2012
Made in U.S.A.

with permission by
Blake Education
Locked Bag 2022
Glebe NSW 2037

Contents

Contents *(cont.)*

Introduction

This first book of *Grammar Practice* for first and second grades provides teachers with resources, activities, and ideas aimed at introducing students to the basic elements of grammar. The activity pages can be used as a resource around which to build and develop a classroom program.

Good grammar skills help children improve their expression and give them an appreciation of how the various elements of English are used to convey meaning. With an understanding of the rules, processes, and elements that govern English, children are able to communicate both correctly and effectively.

In the past, lessons in grammar often became irrelevant and meaningless to students because of the tendency to stress the elements rather than focus on the functions of the elements. *Grammar Practice* ensures that the functions of elements such as parts of speech, phrases, and sentences are related to expression in a practical and purposeful way.

Grammar Practice is designed to make it as easy as possible to find what you need. Photocopiable work sheets are grouped according to grammatical element, and each of these elements is introduced with a definition and examples for the teacher, followed by a collection of appropriate and motivating teaching strategies.

Also included at the end of this book are review work sheets which cover both of the two main sections—"Parts of Speech" and "Composition." All the review activities are directly related to the preceding lessons. Finally, there is an answer key that is included to make the use of the *Grammar Practice* work sheets easier and more efficient. With the three books in *Grammar Practice*, teachers can create an individual and comprehensive grammar program for their students.

How to Use This Book

The *Grammar Practice* series aims to improve children's ability to
- **use language effectively in their own writing,**
- **use language accurately in their own writing,**
- **read critically the writing of others.**

With this in mind, the books have been designed to make it easy for teachers to find the following:

The grammatical elements to teach at each level
- Refer to the overview provided by the assessment checklist.
- Read the background information to find the terminology and depth of treatment appropriate.

Concise background information about each grammatical element
- This is located in the introduction to each grammatical element.

Practical strategies showing how to teach each grammatical element
- Use clever activities as starting points to introduce a grammatical element and capture children's interest.
- Use other proven strategies to explicitly teach or model a grammatical element.
- Use games for reinforcement.

Blackline master (BLM) work sheets to reinforce learning
- They are a comprehensive resource around which to build a program.

Systematic teaching

Children need a solid general framework of grammatical understanding and skills to support their learning across the curriculum. To provide this framework, you may want to teach certain grammatical elements in a systematic way. The assessment checklists provided in each level of *Grammar Practice* indicate the grammatical elements that students should understand by the end of each level. The checklists can be used to program your systematic teaching and to record children's achievements.

For example, using the Assessment Checklist in this book, you can coordinate the "question, statement, exclamation, command" section under "Sentences" with the "question marks," "exclamation marks," and "quotation marks" sections under "Punctuation." Numerous ideas for lessons covering both sentences and end punctuation are in Teaching Strategies, and BLM work sheets for end punctuation are available for you to use with your students.

How to Use This Book *(cont.)*

Incidental teaching

Incidental teaching is an important strategy to use to help students build on prior learning and develop their understanding of grammar in context. A grammar lesson might, therefore, stem from the context of different texts children are reading and writing or from the need to deal with a specific problem individual children or groups of children are experiencing in their own writing. To teach at this point of need, simply dip into *Grammar Practice* and find the appropriate information, strategies, or work sheets for your children.

For example, if a significant number of your students seem to be having difficulty with the correct use of pronouns, you can go directly to the "Pronouns" section of this book. Several ideas for pronouns lessons are in Teaching Strategies, and BLM pronouns work sheets are available for you to use with your students.

Assessment

To be successful, any grammar program must be accompanied by regular assessment. The methods used may differ from teacher to teacher but should encompass basic points.

For each student, assessment should accomplish the following:

(a) record clearly the progress being made;
(b) indicate the future steps being planned for reinforcement and extension;
(c) indicate specific areas of difficulty and possible remediation;
(d) use various strategies to determine whether an outcome has been achieved;
(e) be a relevant and careful measurement of the stage of grammar development;
(f) provide clear and precise suggestions to parents as to how they may best assist at home;
(g) provide clear and precise information to teachers.

Assessment Checklist

Name _____   Quarter

Parts of Speech	1	2	3	4
Identifies and uses correctly				
nouns as naming words				
proper nouns				
action verbs				
thinking and feeling verbs				
simple past, present, and future tenses				
adjectives as describing words				
adverbs to tell when, where, why, and how				
articles *a, an,* and *the*				
prepositions as place words				
personal and possessive pronouns				
conjunctions to link ideas				

Sentences	1	2	3	4
Identifies and writes				
correct word order in a sentence				
question, statement, exclamation, command				
phrases and clauses				
simple, compound, and complex sentences				

Punctuation	1	2	3	4
Uses				
space between words				
capital letters, periods				
Experiments with				
question marks				
exclamation marks				
commas				
quotation marks				

Comments

Areas of strength _____

Areas of difficulty _____

Steps being undertaken to reinforce areas of difficulty or extend grammar skills

Parts of Speech

Every name is called a **noun**,
As *fence* and *flower*, *street* and *town*;

In place of noun the **pronoun** stands,
As *he* and *she* can raise their hands;

The **adjective** describes a thing,
As *magic* wand and *twisted* string;

The **verb** means action, something done—
To *read* and *write*, to *jump* and *run*;

How things are done the **adverbs** tell,
As *quickly*, *slowly*, *badly*, *well*;

The **preposition** shows the place,
As *in* the street or *at* the base;

Conjunctions join, in many ways,
Sentences, words, *or* phrase *and* phrase.

anonymous

Nouns

Introduction

First and second grade students should be made familiar with the following functions of a **noun**.

(a) Nouns are the **names** of things around us. Nouns that are used to name general things (rather than a particular person or thing) are called **common nouns**.
Examples: *dog, table, car, bottle*

(b) Some nouns are the names of particular or special people or things. These are called **proper nouns** and are written with a capital letter at the beginning.
Examples: *Katy, Ben, October, United States, North Carolina, Christopher Columbus*

(c) Some nouns are the names we use for collections of things. These are called **collective nouns**.
Examples: *flock* of birds, *herd* of cattle, *bunch* of grapes

(d) Nouns have **number**. They can mean one thing or more than one thing.
Examples: *one bird, two birds, the dog, the dogs*

Children should also be introduced to the relationship of nouns to words such as verbs (words that tell what the noun is doing), adjectives (words that describe the noun), and pronouns (words that take the places of nouns).

Teaching Strategies

Where's the thing?

Have children come to understand the function of a noun by asking them to bring you items which you refer to only as "things."
Mark, please bring me the thing from the table. . . . No! No! I want the other thing.
The ensuing confusion will soon have children asking you questions. Through guided discussion you can show them the importance of everything having a name so that we can communicate our thoughts clearly.

Mystery bag

Fill a cloth bag with a variety of small objects. Have children guess the names of items that they think you have hidden in it. You may want to write their guesses on the chalkboard. After awhile, have them feel the bag to see if they can identify any objects. Write the names of the things they have identified on the chalkboard.

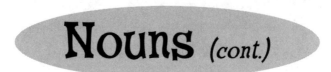

Nouns (cont.)

Name quiz

Conduct a name quiz by giving children clues about a certain object and having them guess what it is.

I am a book. I have lots of words in me. My name begins with d.
I tell you what words mean. (dictionary)

Listing

Challenge children to write or say, in a set time, a set number of nouns in a certain category.

Name ten types of birds. (sparrow, dove, emu . . .)
Name ten children in this grade. (Chan, Mike, Sally . . .)

Alphabet game

Choose a letter of the alphabet and challenge children to write the names of as many things as they can that begin with that letter. This can be played as a circle game, with each successive child in the circle adding a new name.

s—snake, stove, sky, sandal . . .

Cloze exercises

These are excellent for the study of nouns in context. They are best made up by the class teacher and do not need to be long or complex. Correct children's efforts through class discussion.

Mike rode his _____ to school today. It has two _____ . The _____ is so high that Mike can hardly touch the pedals.

Noun cutouts

Allow children to search through newspapers and magazines, cutting out pictures of things they like or don't like. Then have them paste the pictures on a sheet, grouped under the headings "Things I Like" and "Things I Don't Like." Finally, have them write the name of each thing underneath its picture.

WORD BANK   Nouns

Common Nouns

ant	cup	hut	pan
bag	dad	jet	peg
bed	day	jug	pen
box	dog	leg	pet
boy	egg	lip	pig
bug	fan	log	pup
bun	fig	man	rat
bus	fin	map	rib
can	fog	mat	rod
cap	fox	men	sun
cat	gas	mom	tap
cog	hat	mud	vet
cot	ham	net	war
cow	hen	nut	wig

Proper Nouns

Ben	Sunday	Thursday	Los Angeles
Lake Placid	Monday	Friday	New York
Lisa	Tuesday	Saturday	Bambi
Pacific Ocean	Wednesday	December	Mars

Collective Nouns

bunch	pod	jury	crowd
herd	school	team	class
flock	litter	crew	family

Common Nouns

Nouns are the names of things around us.

Fill in the missing letters to complete the names.

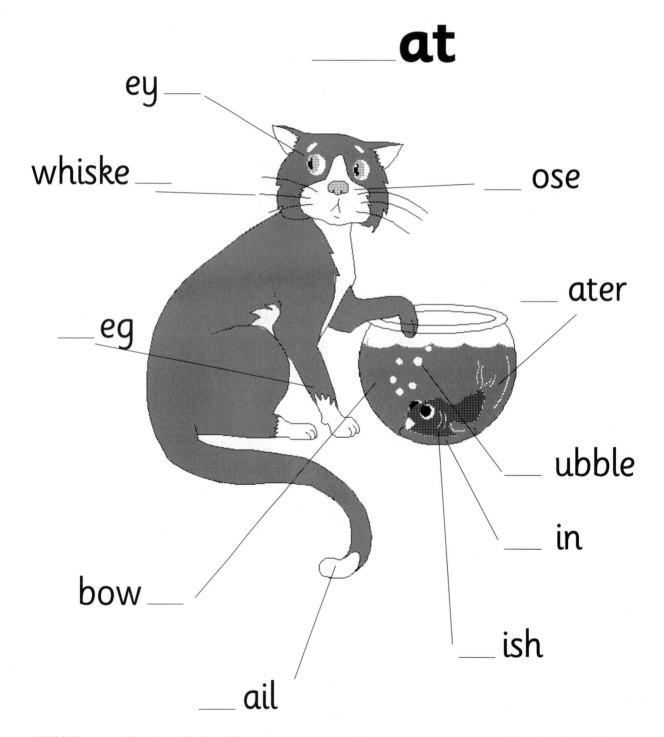

___ **at**

ey ___

whiske ___

___ ose

___ eg

___ ater

bow ___

___ ubble

___ in

___ ish

___ ail

Common Nouns

Name _____ Grammar BLM **2**

Nouns are the names of things around us.

Fill in the missing letters to complete the names.

_____ **og**

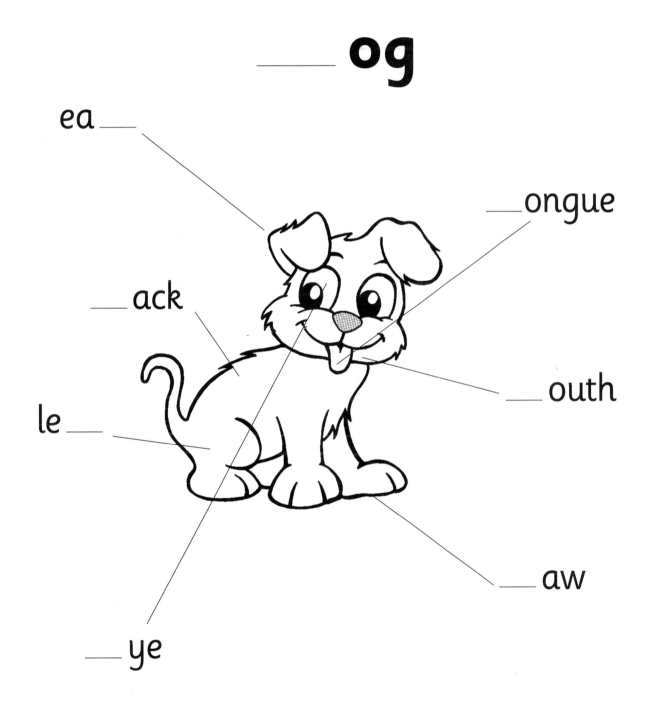

ea _____

_____ongue

_____ack

_____outh

le _____

_____aw

_____ye

Common Nouns

Name _____ Grammar BLM **3**

Nouns are the names of things around us.
Write the correct animal name in each space.

tiger   giraffe   camel

mouse   horse   zebra

a. A _____ has a hump.

b. A _____ eats cheese.

c. A _____ has a very long neck.

d. A _____ has black and yellow stripes.

e. A _____ has black and white stripes.

f. We can ride a _____.

Common Nouns

Nouns are the names of things around us.

Color the boxes that contain the names of things you can see in the picture.

window	donkey	broom
apple	bus	bucket
train	box	flower
car	truck	bicycle
bug	crab	table

Common Nouns

Nouns are the names of things around us.

1. Color farm animals red.
   Color zoo animals blue.

2. Color the names of things that have legs.

truck	girl	bus
bird	car	tiger
table	man	bug
boat	bike	chair

Common Nouns

Name _____ Grammar BLM **6**

Nouns are the names of things around us.

Use a name from the box to solve each puzzle.

egg	car	star	cow

a. I have horns.

I eat grass.

I give milk.

I am a _____.

c. I have a shell.

Birds lay me.

I am yellow and white inside.

I am an _____.

b. I am high up in the sky.

I twinkle at night.

I am a _____.

d. I have wheels and doors.

Inside I have seats.

I take people places.

I am a _____.

Common Nouns

Nouns are the names of things around us.

Find the name for each picture. Write it on the line.

b	o	o	k	b
t	e	n	t	o
s	h	i	p	x
c	r	i	n	g
o	b	a	b	y
w	d	u	c	k

 _____    _____

 _____    _____

 _____   _____

 _____    _____

Common Nouns

Name _____   Grammar BLM   **8**

Nouns are the names of things around us.
Complete each set of nouns (names) with one of these words.

> eagle   apple   ant   star   mother
> sofa   lamb   shovel

a. grasshopper, bee, wasp, _____

b. moon, sun, comet, _____

c. cherry, grape, pear, _____

d. robin, blackbird, crow, _____

e. hoe, fork, rake, _____

f. puppy, calf, kitten, _____

g. bed, chair, table, _____

h. father, sister, brother, _____

Proper Nouns

Proper nouns are names of special people, places, or things. They always start with a capital letter.

Add a word from the box to complete each sentence.

December	Tuesday	Joanne
New York City	Terry	Spot

a. My best friend at school is a girl called

_____ .

b. My birthday is next_____ .

c. Christmas is in _____ .

d. My small black and white dog is called

_____ .

e. My dad's name is _____ .

f. A large city in the United States is called

_____ .

Proper Nouns

Name _____   Grammar BLM **10**

Proper nouns are names of special people, places, or things. They always start with a capital letter.

Fill in the blank space. The proper nouns in the stars will help you.

Sunday

Monday

Tuesday

Wednesday

Thursday

Friday

Saturday

a. The second day of the week is

_____.

b. The day before Thursday is

_____.

c. The day after Wednesday is

_____.

d. The first day of the week is

_____.

e. The two days that make up the

weekend are _____

and _____.

Collective Nouns

Collective nouns name a collection of people or things.
Choose a collective noun to name each drawing.

forest	bunch	swarm	herd
flock	litter	team	fleet

a. a _____ of bees

b. a _____ of birds

c. a _____ of grapes

d. a _____ of elephants

e. a _____ of ships

f. a _____ of soccer players

g. a _____ of puppies

h. a _____ of trees

Singular and Plural Nouns

Name _____   Grammar BLM   **12**

Nouns can be singular (one) or plural (more than one).
Look at the pictures. Fill in the missing words.

a. one cow   two _____

b. one book   three _____

c. one dog   two _____

d. one chair   two _____

e. one ring   two _____

f . one tree   three _____

g. one _____   five cats

h. one _____   three flowers

i. one _____   two horses

Singular and Plural Nouns

Nouns can be singular (one) or plural (more than one).
Write the correct word in each space.

goose geese	man men
foot feet	woman women
tooth teeth	child children

a. two _____

b. one _____

c. three _____

d. two _____

e. one _____

f. two _____

Verbs

Introduction

Through informal activities and class discussion, first and second grade students should come to understand that a **verb** is a word that expresses an action. Children at this age might find it more accessible to use everyday terminology, such as **doing words** or **action words**.

Children need to develop an awareness of the following types of verbs and their uses.

(a) **Doing verbs** are words that express a concrete action. They are common in spoken language and in the writing of young children.
Examples: *work, run, sit, eat, jump*

(b) **Saying verbs** express a spoken action.
Examples: *talk, tell, said, suggested, yelled*

(c) Some verbs do not express a concrete action—they express actions that happen mentally, such as feelings, ideas, thoughts, or attitudes. These can be called **thinking and feeling verbs**. They are common in arguments, narratives, and descriptions (but not scientific descriptions, which are objective).
Examples: I *like* Sam. I *understand*. Katy *believed* the story.
   I *see* the rabbit. I *think* people should recycle.

(d) Some verbs tell us about what things are and what they have. These are **being and having verbs**. They are common in all kinds of descriptions.
Examples: Ben *is* a good swimmer. Ali *has* the answer. They *are* here.
   (*Is, are, has,* and *have* can also act as auxiliary or helping verbs for doing, thinking, and feeling verbs. Example: Ben *is swimming*.)

A verb is the key around which a sentence is built, and children need to be shown the importance of choosing the most expressive verb when speaking or writing.

At this level, children should also be given constant informal practice in the correct use of certain verbs which are often misused.

Examples:	*went—gone*	*may—can*
	seen—saw	*swim—swam*
	did—done	*broke—broken*
	came—come	*learn—teach*
	was—were	*sing—sung*

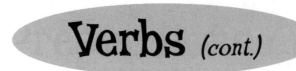

Verbs (cont.)

Teaching Strategies

Get active

Call for volunteers to perform certain actions and then describe what they are doing. Write what they say on the chalkboard and have other children underline the word(s) that expresses the action.

I am jumping on the spot.

I am hitting the door.

Mime time

Have selected children mime certain actions and challenge the rest of the class to guess what they are doing. Write the guesses on the chalkboard and have children underline the words that express the actions.

Are you sweeping the floor?

Are you milking a cow?

Verb list

Provide children with a suitable noun and then have them add a number of verbs saying what that noun does.

A snake bites and hisses.

A horse gallops and neighs.

Vague verbs

Have students suggest more descriptive synonyms for certain verbs such as *walk*. Make lists to post in the classroom so students can refer to them while they are studying verbs and composing sentences.

walk	run	say
stroll	*trot*	*exclaim*
limp	*race*	*whisper*
shuffle	*lope*	*snarl*

Correct it

Tell children a sentence with an incorrect use of a verb. Have them orally correct it.

The boys have went.	*The boys have gone.*
Can I get a drink, please?	*May I get a drink, please?*

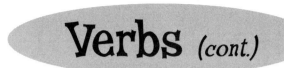

Verbs (cont.)

Verb match

Create two sets of labels—one set with names written on them, the other with matching verbs. Attach the labels to the chalkboard and have children sort them into matching pairs.

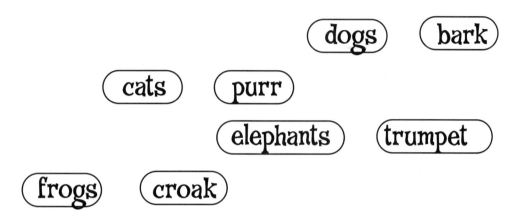

Picture search

Have children search through old magazines and newspapers to find pictures in which an action is taking place. Then have them paste the chosen pictures on a large sheet of paper and beside each picture write a sentence describing the action.

The lady is driving the car.

The man is hitting the golf ball.

I can

Ask children to demonstrate what they can do, describing it aloud as they do it.

I can hop.

I can jump.

I can read.

WORD BANK

Verbs

add	fly	pat
am	get	play
are	go	put
ask	goes	ran
be	going	ride
bit	got	rub
bite	had	run
bump	has	sat
call	have	saw
can	hear	see
come	hid	sing
cry	hit	sip
cut	hop	sit
did	hug	stop
do	is	take
does	jog	tell
done	jump	use
eat	keep	walk
fall	let	want
fed	look	was
feed	met	went
feel	mix	were
fell	mop	wish
find	nip	woke

Verbs

Verbs are doing words or action words.
Fill in the missing letters to complete the doing words.

I can ____ op.

I can _____ un.

I can _____ ow.

I can _____ ide.

I can _____ leep.

I can _____ ance.

I can _____ ly.

I can _____ ish.

Nouns and Verbs

Name _____   Grammar BLM **15**

Nouns are the names of things around us.
Verbs are doing words or action words.
Look at the pictures and names. Then answer the questions.

clock    a. What swims? _____

fish   b. What quacks? _____

dog   c. What sails? _____

horse    d. What falls? _____

duck   e. What trots? _____

rain   f. What ticks? _____

boat      g. What barks? _____

Nouns and Verbs

Name _____   Grammar BLM   **16**

Nouns are the names of things around us.
Verbs are doing words or action words.

Add a verb from the first box and a noun from the second box to complete each sentence. The first one has been done for you.

```
                    Verbs
   build     read     cut     kick     boil     wear
```

```
                    Nouns
   eggs   bread   coat   sandcastle   ball   book
```

a. Ian can ___**kick**___ a ___**ball**___ over the fence.

b. Sally can _____ a _____ about dinosaurs.

c. Joanne can _____ some _____ in a pot.

d. I like to _____ a _____ on a cold day.

e. Kathy can _____ a _____ at the beach.

f. Mike can _____ the _____ with a knife.

Nouns and Verbs

Name _____   Grammar BLM **17**

Nouns are the names of things around us.
Verbs are doing words or action words.

Look at each sentence. Find the noun (naming word) and write it in the box. Find the verb (doing word) and write it in the box.

a. The sun shines.

b. The fish swims.

c. The wind blows.

d. A duck quacks.

e. The rain falls.

f. A horse trots.

Noun (naming word)

Verb (doing word)

Nouns and Verbs

Name _____   Grammar BLM **18**

Nouns are the names of things around us.
Verbs are doing words or action words.
Find the correct verb for each sentence. Write it on the line.

h	b	a	r	k
o	f	l	y	r
p	c	r	y	i
s	w	i	m	n
t	i	c	k	g

a. A bird can _____.

b. A dog can _____.

c. A frog can _____.

d. A baby can _____.

e. A fish can _____.

f. A bell can _____.

g. A clock can _____.

Verbs

Verbs are doing words or action words.

1. Color the verbs (action words) that each noun (naming word) can do. The first one has been done for you.

Noun (naming word)	Verbs (action words)			
boy	skip	eat	fly	kick
snake	slither	read	bite	hiss
chicken	drink	eat	shoot	scratch
fish	swim	eat	breathe	grow
dog	talk	eat	bark	play
horse	gallop	grow	eat	fly
duck	swim	fly	quack	bark
fire	burn	heat	cook	wash
wheel	sing	spin	turn	roll

2. Color the ones you can do.

eating	pushing	scratching	buzzing
sleeping	playing	growing	reading
flying	barking	swimming	quacking

3. Write a sentence saying what you like doing best of all.

I like _____

_____.

Verbs

Name _____ Grammar BLM **20**

Verbs are doing words or action words.

Tell what is happening in these pictures. Use action words.

a.    The boy sits.

He is _____ .

b.    The girl throws.

She is _____ .

c.    The clown stands.

He is _____ .

d.   The rain is falling.

The rain _____ .

e.    The bird is flying.

The bird _____ .

f.   Cuddles growls.

He is _____ .

Verbs

Verbs are doing words or action words.

Find the correct verb for each sentence. Write it on the line.

s	w	a	m	l
w	a	t	e	i
a	c	r	y	c
s	s	a	w	k
h	h	o	p	e
t	o	l	d	d

a. The teacher _____ us a story about snakes.

b. The baby will _____ because it is hungry.

c. I _____ her take the pencils.

d. Billy _____ across the river.

e. The cat _____ its fur.

f. Mike will _____ the dog.

g. The kangaroo will _____ the dog.

h. I _____ a pie for lunch.

Verbs

Name _____   Grammar BLM

Verbs are doing words or action words.

Read the story. Put the correct verbs in the spaces.

brushed	washed	ate	put
jumped	said	went	watch

After he _____ his dinner, Billy went to the

bathroom and _____ his hands and _____

his teeth. He then _____ on his pajamas and

_____ into the family room to _____

television. When it was eight o'clock, he _____

goodnight to his mother and then _____ into his bed.

Verbs

Verbs are doing words or action words.

Find the correct verb for each sentence. Write it on the line.

o	p	e	n	e
b	a	k	e	a
t	e	l	l	t
m	a	k	e	s
w	a	s	h	e
p	e	e	l	t

a. We can _____ dirty hands.

b. We can _____ a table.

c. We can _____ a cake.

d. We can _____ a meal.

e. We can _____ a door.

f. We can _____ a story.

g. We can _____ a bed.

h. We can _____ an orange.

Verbs

Verbs are doing words or action words.

Add a verb to each line to make a proper sentence. The first one has been done for you.

a. Lisa the ball

   <u>Lisa kicked the ball.</u> _____

b. The dog at me

   _____

c. Our teacher us a story

   _____

d. The train at the station

   _____

e. The puppy the bone

   _____

f. The kangaroo over the fence

   _____

g. Sally the bell for play

   _____

h. The bird into the tree

   _____

Verbs

Name _____   Grammar BLM **25**

We use *is* when we are talking about one person or thing. We use *are* when we are talking about two or more people or things.

Use the verb is or the verb are to complete each sentence.

a. A rose _____ a flower.

b. The tigers _____ in the jungle.

c. These cakes _____ stale.

d. Elephants _____ large animals.

e. The door _____ open.

f. The dog _____ chewing a bone.

g. The girls _____ playing softball.

h. The kitten _____ playing.

i. Sam and Joe _____ jumping the fence.

j. A lady _____ mowing the lawn.

Verbs

We use *was* when we are talking about one person or thing. We use *were* when we are talking about two or more people or things.

Use the verb was or the verb were to complete each sentence.

a. The horse _____ in the stable.

b. The train _____ late.

c. The windows _____ shut.

d. The apple _____ ripe.

e. The socks _____ dirty.

f. The children _____ sweeping the path.

g. The stars _____ shining last night.

h. She _____ riding the bike.

i. The girl _____ playing badminton.

j. The dogs _____ chasing the cat.

Doing Verbs

Doing verbs are words that express an action you can see.

1. Are you able to see the actions that these sentences are about?
   Circle the doing verb in each one.

    a. I ran to the park.

    b. My sister sat on the swing.

    c. Ian jumped over the fence.

    d. We ate our lunch.

    e. We walked home.

    f. Next time, I rode my bike.

2. On the lines below, tell how you got to school today. Use as many
   doing verbs as you can.

    _____

    _____

    _____

    _____

Thinking and Feeling Verbs

Name _____

Some verbs do not express an action you can see—they express actions that happen mentally, such as feelings and thoughts. These can be called thinking and feeling verbs.

1. Circle the thinking or feeling verb in each sentence.

   a. I like the park.

   b. My sister saw the dog.

   c. Ian thought about his birthday party.

   d. Next time, I believed him.

   e. We hated the walk home.

   f. I think often about that movie.

2. On the lines below, write an argument to convince your parents to take you to the park. Use as many thinking and feeling verbs as you can.

   _____

   _____

   _____

   _____

Present Tense Verbs

Name _____   Grammar BLM **29**

Verbs can show that the action is taking place now. This is called present tense.

1. **Use a verb from the box to complete each sentence in the present tense.**

barks	hits	sweeps
grow	swims	sits

a. Mike _____ the ball.

b. My dog _____ .

c. Sally _____ in a big chair.

d. Joanne _____ the floor.

e. Tomatoes _____ in our garden.

f. Ben _____ in the race.

2. **Choose the correct word to complete each sentence in the present tense.**

a. She _____ an ice cream. **(buys, bought)**

b. Mike _____ seeds in his garden. **(plants, planted)**

c. The cat _____ me. **(scratches, scratched)**

d. You _____ higher than I do. **(jump, jumped)**

Past Tense Verbs

Name _____

Verbs can show that the action has taken place in the past. This is called past tense.

1. **Use a verb from the box to complete each sentence in the past tense.**

> helped   played   dug   broke   ate   dropped

a. We _____ football last Saturday.

b. I _____ my leg when I fell over.

c. Colin _____ a hamburger for lunch.

d. The glass broke when I _____ it.

e. Sally_____ a hole to bury the leaves.

f. I _____ my mother lift the heavy table.

2. **Choose the correct word to complete each sentence in the past tense.**

a. It _____ all day. **(rains, rained)**

b. The lamp _____ onto the floor. **(fell, falls)**

c. We _____ to the beach. **(drove, drive)**

d. The dog _____ my brother. **(bites, bit)**

Future Tense Verbs

Name _____

Verbs can show that the action will take place in the future. This is called future tense.

1. **Use a verb from the box to complete each sentence in the future tense. Future tense uses *will* before the main verb.**

> catch   bite   come   eat   begin   break

a. We *will* _____ our lunch after the bell rings.

b. The dog *will* _____ you if you tease it.

c. The glass *will* _____ if you drop it.

d. Mike *will* _____ after he finishes his homework.

e. We *will* _____ lots of fish tomorrow.

f. The concert *will* _____ very soon.

2. **Choose the correct word to complete each sentence in the future tense.**

a. I *will* _____ in this room. **(hid, hide)**

b. We *will* _____ shortly. **(go, went)**

c. Sam *will* _____ lift the boxes. **(help, helped)**

d. Mike *will* _____ the race easily. **(win, won)**

Adjectives

Introduction

Adjectives are words that tell us more about nouns or pronouns by describing them, adding detail, or refining their meanings. First and second grade students can refer to adjectives as **describing words**.

By using adjectives, we can add meaning and interest to sentences.

Examples: The *kind* girl showed the *old* lady the way.
The *savage* dog chased the *frightened* boy.
The *playful* dog chased the *laughing* boy.
The *rude* girl shoved the *disabled* lady.

Children should be encouraged to think about the adjectives they choose and to steer away from adjectives that have become meaningless through overuse, such as "nice" and "good."

Examples: It was a *nice* day. It was a *sunny* day.
That was a *good* story. That was an *exciting* story.

Like "nice" and "good," these are also considered overused adjectives that should be replaced with more exact choices: *fine, grand, funny, awful, lovely, terrible, crazy, adorable, sweet, cool, cute.*

Teaching Strategies
Describe the picture

Display a large poster to the class. Have children orally describe the different objects and people featured in the picture.

What color is the bird?   *The bird is yellow.*
What type of tree is it?   *It is a big, shady tree.*
What colors are the flowers?   *They are purple and red.*

Character words

After reading a story to children, ask them to provide describing words for the characters.

What kind of person was Cinderella?
What words could we use to describe the ugly stepsisters?
What adjectives will help paint a picture of the prince?

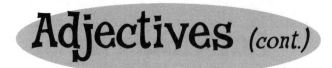

Adjectives (cont.)

Describe the noun

Have children suggest adjectives to describe nouns you have written on the chalkboard. Children could work in groups to compile lists of adjectives and then compare their lists with those of another group.

dog   *savage, big, friendly, black, loyal . . .*
teacher
car
pupil
bike

Follow the instructions

Give children a piece of paper and have them follow your instructions to draw a noun modified by an adjective.

Draw a fat pig.
Draw a tall boy.
Draw a yellow roof.
Draw a happy girl.
Draw a fast boat.

Oral adjectives

Challenge children to orally supply adjectives for nouns you have written on the chalkboard.

A teacher should be _____ and_____ .
A football player should be_____ and_____ .

Opposites

Have children supply the opposite of an adjective you have given in a sentence.

An elephant is large but a mouse is . . .
A fire is hot but ice is . . .

A nice challenge

Challenge children to create lists of adjectives that are more meaningful than "nice" or "good." These could be displayed around the classroom for future reference.

a nice day   a sunny day, an enjoyable day . . .
a good dog   a loyal dog, an obedient dog . . .

WORD BANK

Adjectives

a	dry	red
all	every	rich
an	fat	short
any	fit	shy
bad	good	small
bent	green	soft
best	hot	strong
big	kind	the
black	lazy	thick
brown	little	tidy
cool	new	white
deep	no	wide
dirty	old	wise

Adjectives

Name _____

Adjectives are describing words. They are used to describe nouns (naming words).

Circle the adjective that best describes the underlined noun.

a. A <u>canary</u> is (yellow, black) and white.

b. A <u>pig</u> can be (fat, dry).

c. <u>Grass</u> is usually (green, clean).

d. A <u>circle</u> is always (square, round).

e. A ripe <u>apple</u> is sometimes (red, blue).

f. <u>Feathers</u> are usually (left, soft).

g. An <u>elephant</u> is a very (strong, long) animal.

h. A savage <u>tiger</u> is (wild, mild).

i. <u>Clowns</u> are usually (angry, funny).

j. A <u>crow</u> is (black, pink).

50

Adjectives

Adjectives are describing words. They are used to describe nouns (naming words).

Underline the nouns. Circle the adjectives. Then color the picture.

a. The grass is green.

b. The flowers are red.

c. The horse is black.

d. The house is brown.

e. The pond is blue.

f. The ducks are yellow.

Adjectives

Name _____   Grammar BLM 34

Adjectives are describing words. They are used to describe nouns (naming words).

Underline the nouns. Circle the adjectives. (Articles [*a, an, the*] are adjectives.) Then follow the instructions to draw the picture.

a. Draw two trees on a hill.

b. Draw a big bird in one tree.

c. Draw a long tail on the big bird.

d. Draw a small lizard under the second tree.

e. Draw a black ant on the small lizard's nose.

Adjectives

Name _____   Grammar BLM **35**

Adjectives are describing words. They are used to describe nouns (naming words).

Use a word from the box to complete each sentence.

low	high	big	small	hot	cold

a. The elephant is _____.

The mouse is _____.

b. The fire is _____.

The icy treat is _____.

c. The teapot is _____.

The girl is _____.

Adjectives

Name _____   Grammar BLM **36**

Adjectives are describing words. They are used to describe nouns (naming words).

1. Color the adjectives (describing words) that can describe each of the nouns (naming words). The first one has been done for you.

Noun (naming word)	Adjectives (describing words)			
banana	**ripe**	sharp	wild	**yellow**
girl	deep	clever	young	empty
knife	sharp	soft	rich	blunt
pillow	healthy	angry	soft	white
dress	pretty	dirty	sharp	loud
pig	square	pink	fat	deep
door	blunt	open	shut	sharp
grass	green	tall	open	fast

2. Circle the adjectives. Then write *yes* or *no* after each sentence.

   a. A mouse can jump over a high wall. _____

   b. An ant has fifteen legs. _____

   c. The earth's moon is made of blue cheese. _____

   d. A dirty, wrinkled jumper needs washing. _____

Adjectives

Adjectives are describing words. They are used to describe nouns (naming words).

Add adjectives in the spaces below. Then draw pictures to match your descriptions.

a. a _____ _____ apple	b. a _____ _____ house
c. a _____ _____ pencil	d. a _____ _____ tree

Adjectives

Adjectives are describing words. They are used to describe nouns (naming words).

1. **Choose an adjective from the box to fill each space.**

| ripe   tiny   large   greedy   tall   deep |

One day a _____ elephant met a _____

mouse near a _____ river. The mouse was eating a

_____ banana it had found under a _____

tree. The _____ elephant stole the banana from the

mouse.

2. **Think of a better adjective to replace "nice" in each space.**

    a. a nice shape   a _____ shape

    b. a nice dress   a _____ dress

    c. a nice table   a _____ table

    d. a nice day   a _____ day

Adjectives

Adjectives are describing words. They are used to describe nouns (naming words).

1. **The words in the box are jumbled. Rearrange the letters to make adjectives to fill the spaces below.**

> itewh   wto   eepd   enw   tfos

   a. A zebra has black and _____stripes.

   b. A shallow pool is not _____ .

   c. There are _____ dogs in the kennel.

   d. Rock is hard, but wool is _____ .

   e. Have you seen their _____ car?

2. **Choose an adjective that has a similar meaning to the underlined adjective in each sentence.**

> damp   warm   tiny   fast   big

   a. This is a <u>small</u> mouse. This is a _____ mouse.

   b. The sun is <u>hot</u>. The sun is _____ .

   c. This shirt is <u>wet</u>. This shirt is _____ .

   d. Tom is <u>quick</u>. Tom is _____ .

   e. This table is <u>large</u>. This table is _____ .

Adverbs

Introduction

An **adverb** is a word that adds meaning to a verb, an adjective, or another adverb. It tells **when, where,** or **how**. First and second grade students can refer to adverbs as **when, where,** or **how words**.

Examples: We went to the movies *yesterday*. (when)
Put it over *there*. (where)
The dog barked *loudly*. (how)

Adverbs help us add important detail to the meaning of a sentence. Take the example "Bill *went* to the door." We can add to the verb *went* such words as *slowly, quickly, lazily, hastily.*

A large number of adverbs are formed from adjectives by adding *-ly*. Most of the "how" words end in *-ly*.

Examples: *quickly*   *beautifully*   *quietly*   *slowly*   *really*
heavily   *angrily*   *neatly*   *greedily*   *eagerly*

Not all adverbs end in *-ly*.

Examples: *fast*   *soon*   *more*   *less*   *now*
then   *here*   *there*   *far*   *near*
late   *today*   *tomorrow*   *yesterday*

Not all words which end in *-ly* are adverbs, Some of them are adjectives because they are used to describe or limit nouns or pronouns.

Examples: *friendly*   *lovely*   *only*   *ghostly*
ugly   *womanly*   *saintly*   *likely*

Be sure to see whether the *-ly* word is about a noun or pronoun or about an adjective, a verb, or an adverb.

Teaching Strategies

Add an adverb

Begin a sentence and have children orally add an adverb. Encourage them to try to think of a when, where, and how word for each sentence.

The cat ran . . . today (when), here (where), quickly (how).

How, when, or where?

Ask children to decide what a particular adverb tells us.

The children sang sweetly. Sweetly tells us how the children sang.

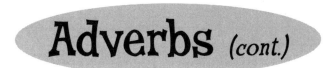

Adverbs *(cont.)*

Act it how?

Ask for volunteers to act out the action of a verb in different ways. Have the rest of the class supply a *how* word to match the acting out.

She hopped (quickly, slowly, clumsily, noisily, quietly) across the classroom.

Verb/adverb pairs

Organize children in pairs. Have one partner say a verb and the other provide a suitable adverb (when, where, or how word). Swap roles. To make the game more challenging, have children provide a when, where, and how word for each verb.

Child 1: ran   *Child 2: quickly*
Child 2: played   *Child 1: happily*

Adjective or adverb?

Prepare short chalkboard exercises in which children must distinguish between the adjective and the adverb—and choose the adverb as being correct.

The dog barked   *(loud, loudly).*
The children played   *(happily, happy).*

Presto chango

Students can learn about the relationships among words by changing adverbs into adjectives. They can "test" the words they work with by trying them out with verbs and nouns or pronouns.

adverbs + verbs

He *neatly fixed* it.

He *happily played* it.

He *easily won* it.

He *suddenly fell.*

He *swiftly ran.*

He *hardly works.*

adjectives + nouns

She is a *neat person.*

She is a *happy child.*

She had an *easy problem.*

She made a *sudden escape.*

She is a *swift runner.*

She is a *hard worker.*

WORD BANK

Adverbs

again	loudly	softly
all	more	then
as	neatly	there
at	no	today
back	not	too
by	now	very
early	often	well
far	out	what
fast	quickly	when
here	rather	where
how	sadly	why
in	since	yes
last	slowly	yet
late	so	yonder

Adverbs

Adverbs are words that tell us *when* something is done, *where* something is done, or *how* something is done.

When did you run?	**I ran *today*.**
Where did you run?	**I ran *here*.**
How did you run?	**I ran *quickly*.**

1. **Look at the underlined word in each sentence. Does it tell you *when*, *where*, or *how*? Write *when*, *where*, or *how* on the line.**

    a. We will go <u>tomorrow</u>. _____

    b. He runs <u>quickly</u>. _____

    c. Put the box over <u>there</u>. _____

    d. I want you to do it <u>today</u>. _____

    e. Trees grow <u>slowly</u>. _____

    f. We all ran over <u>there</u>. _____

2. **What do these words tell us? Write *when*, *where*, or *how* on each line.**

    a. soon _____

    b. tomorrow _____

    c. fast _____

    d. here _____

    e. there _____

    f. early _____

    g. slowly _____

Adverbs

Adverbs are words that tell us _when_ something is done, _where_ something is done, or _how_ something is done.

When did you run?	**I ran _today_.**
Where did you run?	**I ran _here_.**
How did you run?	**I ran _quickly_.**

Add a word from the box to tell when, where, or how.

softly   early   still   often   hard   there   here   tonight

a. He stood _____ . (how)

b. Mike arrived _____ . (when)

c. She sang_____ . (how)

d. She put it_____ . (where)

e. She tried very _____ . (how)

f. I have been to Chicago _____ . (when)

g. He lost his watch right _____ . (where)

h. We will see the moon _____ . (when)

Adverbs

Adverbs are words that tell us *when* something is done, *where* something is done, or *how* something is done.

When did you run?	I ran *today*.
Where did you run?	I ran *here*.
How did you run?	I ran *quickly*.

1. **Choose from the box an adverb that has an opposite meaning to the underlined adverb.**

> later   late   there   inside   down

   a. He will arrive <u>soon</u>.   _____

   b. Mike arrived <u>early</u>.   _____

   c. Sally stopped <u>here</u>.   _____

   d. I looked <u>up</u>.   _____

   e. He stayed <u>outside</u>.   _____

2. **Draw lines to match each word to the underlined words it could replace.**

   a. She arrived <u>before it was late</u>.   now

   b. I ran <u>very fast</u>.   early

   c. She sang <u>in a soft voice</u>.   before

   d. I have seen that movie <u>another time</u>.   quickly

   e. I want to do it <u>straight away</u>.   softly

Adverbs

Adverbs are words that tell us *when* something is done, *where* something is done, or *how* something is done.

When did you run?	I ran *today*.
Where did you run?	I ran *here*.
How did you run?	I ran *quickly*.

1. Write sentences using these *when* words.

a. yesterday

_____

b. now

_____

2. Write sentences using these *where* words.

a. out

_____

b. near

_____

3. Write sentences using these *how* words.

a. noisily

_____

b. slowly

_____

Adverbs

Name _____   Grammar BLM **44**

Adverbs are words that tell us *when* something is done, *where* something is done, or *how* something is done.

When did you run?	**I ran *today*.**
Where did you run?	**I ran *here*.**
How did you run?	**I ran *quickly*.**

Choose the correct word to fill each space.

a. (strong, strongly)

The wind blew _____.

adverb

Mike is a _____ boy.

adjective

b. (quick, quickly)

Tom ran _____ across the yard.

adverb

Susan is a _____ runner.

adjective

c. (slow, slowly)

Tom was too _____ to win the race.

adjective

The lazy girl walked _____ across the yard.

adverb

d. (sad, sadly)

Mike is a very _____ boy today.

adjective

The young girl cried _____.

adverb

Articles

Introduction

First and second grade students need practice using the **articles** *the, a,* and *an* appropriately. Articles can be either definite or indefinite.

(a) *The* is the **definite article**. It is definite because it is referring to a specific thing.

Examples: *The* man lives next door. *The* dog is outside.

(b) *A* and *an* are **indefinite articles**. Rather than referring to a specific thing, they refer to any one of a group of things.

Examples: *A* man lives next door. *A* dog is outside.

An is used instead of *a* in front of words that begin with a vowel (a, e, i, o, u). *An* is also used in front of words that begin with a silent *h.*

Examples: *an* apple, *an* egg, *an* igloo, *an* orange, *an* umbrella, *an* hour but *a* hotel

Teaching Strategies

Playing alphabet games will help primary children to readily identify vowels—and thus use *a* or *an* appropriately.

Fish for the letter

Make up small cards with the letters of the alphabet written on them. Have children play "Go fish!" with them.

Alphabet quiz

Write the alphabet across the chalkboard and conduct an alphabet quiz.

What letter comes before d?

What letter comes after m?

How does it start?

Write the alphabet on the chalkboard. Say a word aloud to the children and then ask a volunteer to come to the board and circle the first letter of the word you said.

Letter hunt

Challenge children to write down all the objects in the classroom that begin with a chosen letter.

f—fish, floor, feet, flower

Articles (cont.)

I spy a vowel

Allow children to play "I Spy" in groups but limit their letter choices to the five vowels and possibly the silent *h*.

The missing article

Write simple sentences on the chalkboard. Have children add *a* or *an*.

I saw   duck.
I saw   apple.

What does it mean?

On the chalkboard write a passage from a story, but leave out the articles. Have children decide whether to use *the* or *a/an* in the spaces. Discuss how the use of *the* or *a/an* changes the meaning.

One day ____ duck found ____ piece of bread under ____ tree.

Article noun test

The articles—a, an, the—can be used to determine whether or not a word is a noun. If a word makes sense or can be used in a sentence with an article before it, it can function as a noun. Because many words in our language can be used as more than one part of speech, the article noun test is a helpful tool.

Have students apply the article noun test to the words in the verb word bank on page 28. Some of those which pass the test are *a fly, the mop, a play, the walk, a jog, the hit, a hug.*

Have them apply the test to the words in the adjective word bank on page 49. These are among those which pass the test: He would not eat *the fat*. They are among *the rich*. That woman is one of *the wise*. Arnold is one of *the fit*.

Even some adverbs from the list on page 60 can be used as nouns: He is among *the late*. She is *the last* of them.

Finally, even some of the words in a list of prepositions can also be used as nouns: *The down* on the newborn duck was soft. She was on *the inside*. They live in *the* great *beyond*.

Articles

The vowels of the alphabet are *a, e, i, o, u*.

1. **Circle the ten words in the box that begin with a vowel.**

bird	egg	axe	door	glass	old	pig	ink
owl	ugly	ice	hat	emu	card	apple	ox

2. **Look at the letters of the alphabet and then answer the questions below.**

a   b   c   d   e   f   g   h   i   j   k   l   m
n   o   p   q   r   s   ts   u   v   w   x   y   z

   a. What letter comes after *k*? _____

   b. What letter comes before *w*? _____

   c. What is the second letter of the alphabet? _____

   d. What is the last letter of the alphabet? _____

   e. What is the next vowel after *e*? _____

   f. What vowel comes between *n* and *p*? _____

Articles

Name _____   Grammar BLM **46**

The vowels of the alphabet are *a, e, i, o, u.* We use *an* instead of *a* in front of words that begin with a vowel sound.

1.   Write a or an in front of each word.

a. _____ boot   g. _____ arm

b. _____ egg   h. _____ ice block

c. _____ fox   i. _____ nose

d. _____ peg   j. _____ drum

e. _____ artist   k. _____ orange

f. _____ ear   l. _____ ox

2.   Write a or an in each space.

a. I saw _____ old car.

b. I have _____ black dog.

c. I climbed _____ oak tree.

d. Sally ate _____ ice cream.

e. The spider ate _____ ant.

f. Mike saw _____ big fire.

g. The story came to _____ end.

h. What _____ ugly monster!

Articles

Name _____   Grammar BLM **47**

The vowels of the alphabet are *a, e, i, o, u*. We use *an* instead of *a* in front of words that begin with a vowel sound.

1. **Color the boxes that contain words that begin with a vowel.**

banana	umbrella	eye
orange	ant	owl
tent	cupboard	table
neck	umpire	elf
ice cream	arm	oven

2. **Write a or an in each space.**

a. _____ olive

b. _____ pear

c. _____ ox

d. _____ tadpole

e. _____ helicopter

f. _____ arrow

g. _____ engine

h. _____ ear

Articles

The vowels of the alphabet are *a, e, i, o, u*. We use *an* instead of *a* in front of words that begin with a vowel sound.

Read the story and then add *a* or *an* in each space.

One day _____ monkey found _____ orange and _____

carrot in _____ old shed. It gave the orange to _____ ape

that was in _____ tree. Then it put the carrot in _____ empty

box so it could eat it later. A little while later _____ hungry fox

found the carrot and took it to its lair under _____ old oak tree

that was growing in _____ farmer's field.

Articles

When we are talking about a particular thing, we use *the*. When we are talking about a general thing, we use *a* or *an*.

1. **Add a word from the box to fill each space. Circle the article.**

> egg   snake   present   book   bone   dog

   a. I saw the _____ bite the man.

   b. Would you like an _____ for breakfast?

   c. Tom gave me a _____ for my birthday.

   d. A _____ was in the kennel.

   e. My dog chewed the _____ I gave it.

   f. I read a _____ yesterday.

2. **Write a, an, or the in each space.**

   a. Sam is _____ fastest runner in the school.

   b. There is _____ girl in my class who has red hair.

   c. Would you like _____ apple?

   d. Tom is _____ best football player in the school.

   e. What _____ interesting story!

   f. Football is _____ rough game.

Prepositions

Introduction

Prepositions are words we use to show the relationship of a noun or a pronoun to another word in the sentence. They can be called **place** words because they often tell us the positions of things.

The puppy is *on* the chair.
The girl is *beside* the chair.
The bone is *under* the chair.

The prepositions *on, beside,* and *under* all refer to the noun *chair.* They tell us the relationship between it and the puppy, the girl, and the bone.

Here are some prepositions students should be made familiar with during the first and second grades.

above	*behind*	*by*	*up*
against	*below*	*down*	*on*
along	*beneath*	*from*	*past*
away	*beside*	*in*	*since*
around	*between*	*into*	*through*
at	*beyond*	*near*	*toward*
off	*under*	*across*	*inside*

Prepositions *(cont.)*

Teaching Strategies

Draw it

On an overhead projector transparency, draw a picture of a table. Ask for volunteers to follow your instructions.

Draw a cat under the table.
Draw an apple on the table.
Draw a dog jumping over the table.
Draw a chair beside the table.
Draw a piece of wood leaning against the table.

Where is it?

Display to children a large picture. Have them explain the positions of certain objects in the picture.

Where is the canary? The canary is in the cage.
Where is the doll? The doll is inside the box.

Follow the instructions

Have children give a friend a series of instructions. The friend must carry out the instructions.

Go to the door. Then put your cap on the table and your schoolbag under the table.

True or false?

Make simple statements about the positions of objects in the classroom. Have children answer "true" or "false."

The clock is above the television set.
The bookcase is behind the door.

Go through it

Have students compose as many prepositional phrases as they can with just one object.

With the object *door*, they could develop several phrases: *through the door, against the door, around the door, at the door, behind the door.*

A live object could also be used: *inside the whale, toward the whale, on the whale, near the whale, beyond the whale.*

Prepositions

Prepositions often tell us the positions of things.

Look at the picture. Then complete each sentence by using a word from the box.

| under   beside   inside   between   above |

a. The cups are _____ the drink bottle.

b. The bread is _____ the cake and the buns.

c. A mouse is crawling _____ the biscuit tin.

d. The can of worms is _____ the drink bottle.

e. The plate is _____ the cake.

Prepositions

Prepositions often tell us the positions of things.

Choose a place word from the box to complete each sentence.

behind	over	into	in	under

a. A cat is _____

the box.

b. The cat is _____

the table.

c. The man is diving _____

the pool.

d. A duck is flying _____

the pond.

e. A pig is standing _____

the wall.

Prepositions

Name _____ Grammar BLM **52**

Prepositions relate one thing to another. They are always followed by a noun or pronoun.

Circle the correct preposition.

a. Mother was angry (**under** **with**) me.

b. Sally jumped (**into** **off**) the water.

c. The box is full (**for** **of**) toys.

d. We buy our apples (**from** **to**) Mr. Jones.

e. Let us wait (**along** **for**) Sally.

f. The cat ran (**under** **in**) the table.

g. The dog was bitten (**by** **with**) a snake.

h. Mary takes a lot of time (**with** **by**) her work.

i. I did not agree (**with** **below**) my teacher.

j. The boy was hit (**by** **of**) a car.

k. Tom is proud (**of** **between**) his little brother.

l. Did they blame you (**for** **under**) the mess?

Prepositions

Name _____ Grammar BLM **53**

Prepositions relate one thing to another. They are always followed by a noun or pronoun.

Circle the prepositions. Then add the better ending to complete each sentence.

a. Tom sailed his boat on _____.

(the leaves   the lake)

b. The boy dived into _____.

(the cold water   the glass jar)

c. The frightened mouse ran under_____.

(the table   an ant)

d. The man tripped and fell down _____.

(the book   the stairs)

e. Would you be afraid of _____?

(a tiger   a ball)

f. We went hiking in_____.
(the forest   the movies)

Prepositions

Name _____   Grammar BLM **54**

Prepositions relate one thing to another. They are always followed by a noun or pronoun.

1. **Circle the prepositions. Then complete each of these sentences in your own words.**

    a. Mr. Smith slipped and fell down _____ .

    b. The boy fell from the tree into _____ .

    c. I saw the cat run behind _____ .

    d. The clock is above _____ .

2. **Look at the pictures. Write *yes* or *no* after each sentence.**

    a. The girl is behind the horse. _____

    b. The rooster is on a fence. _____

    c. The children are behind the swings. _____

    d. The boy is on his bike. _____

Pronouns

Introduction

First and second grade students should be made aware that we use certain words called **pronouns** to take the places of nouns. We do this to avoid repetition when we speak or write.

Young children can easily understand this when introduced to sentences such as these:

> *Bill said that Bill could not come because Bill's father had not bought Bill a new pair of sneakers.*

They can easily see that such a sentence can be written as this:

> *Bill said that he could not come because his father had not bought him a new pair of sneakers.*

Children at this age should be made familiar with the following common pronouns.

Personal pronouns

I	*me*	*we*	*us*
you	*they*	*them*	*it*
she	*he*	*him*	*her*

Possessive personal pronouns

my	*our*	*ours*	*mine*	*your*	*their*
yours	*his*	*hers*	*its*	*theirs*	*her*

Teaching Strategies

Replace the noun

Write sentences on the board and have children suggest pronouns that could replace the nouns.

Mike said that Mike would arrive as soon as Mike's bicycle was fixed.
This bicycle belongs to me. This bicycle is _____.

Hands up

Read a story and have children raise their hands when they hear a pronoun. This can also include nursery rhymes.

Little Miss Muffet,
Sat on *her* tuffet,
Eating *her* curds and whey.

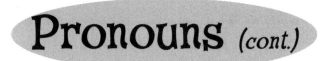
Pronouns (cont.)

Choose the pronoun

Have children choose the correct pronoun to complete a sentence.

Tom said, "Give it back to _____." (me, your)
Did you know _____ goes to Chicago each week? (he, they)

Pronoun cloze

Write a passage on the chalkboard, leaving spaces for the pronouns.
Write the missing pronouns on small pieces of cardboard and have children work in groups to stick them in the correct spaces.

Jane carried the glass to the kitchen. At the sink _____ dropped _____.

Pronoun search

Conduct a pronoun search from a common text, such as a photocopy of a story or poem already read. Have children read the text and circle any pronouns they find.

All about me

Have children write sentences about themselves, using the pronouns *I, me,* or *my.*
I live on a busy street.
My mother gave *me* an ice cream.

Classifying pronouns

To be sure they understand the uses of the personal and possessive personal pronouns, have students classify them according to first person, second person, and third person. Students could then take turns assuming the roles (make signs for them to hold) of first person singular, first person plural, second person singular, second person plural, third person singular, and third person plural and use the pronouns in sentences.

First person *refers to the speaker:*
I, my, mine, me (singular)
we, our, ours, us (plural)

Second person *refers to the person spoken to:*
you, your, yours (same for singular and plural)

Third person *refers to the persons or things spoken about:*
he, his, him, she, her, hers, it, its (singular)
they, their, theirs, them (plural)

Pronouns

Pronouns are words that take the places of nouns.

Rewrite each sentence, replacing the underlined word or words with a word from the box.

> them   it   she   her   he   him

a. Mike said that <u>Mike</u> was the best runner in the school.

_____

b. Sally said that <u>Sally</u> got all her sums correct.

_____

c. The dog barked when the boy hit <u>the dog</u>.

_____

d. The children asked us to wait for <u>the children</u>.

_____

e. Peter asked Tom to give it back to <u>Peter</u>.

_____

f. Mary said that Joanne could come with <u>Mary</u>.

_____

Pronouns

Pronouns are words that take the places of nouns.

1. **Choose a pronoun from the box to fill each space.**

her	they	I	him	me	you

a. Tom is my friend, and I play with _____ each day.

b. I hope _____ am going to win the race tomorrow.

c. "Give_____ back my pencil," said Paul.

d. We saw ten horses, and _____ were all black.

e. Mary gave _____ kitten a bowl of milk.

f. "Do _____ live in this house, Sally?" asked Tom.

2. **Choose the correct pronoun from the box to write in each space in the story.**

them	their	his	we	him	its

Tom and _____ sister Jane went to visit _____ uncle's

farm. Their uncle met _____ at the gate. He had his dog

with _____. The dog had_____ new collar on. Their

uncle said, "Why don't _____ go into the farmhouse for a

cool drink of lemonade?"

Pronouns

Name _____   Grammar BLM **57**

Pronouns are words that take the places of nouns.

1. **In each sentence, circle the word that the underlined pronoun is replacing.**

   a. Mike hit the ball, and then <u>he</u> began to run.

   b. Sally washed the dishes, and then <u>she</u> dried them.

   c. The dog bit the stranger, and then <u>it</u> bit the mailman.

   d. Tom threw the ball to Megan, and <u>she</u> threw it back.

   e. Bill asked for the book, so I gave <u>it</u> to him.

   f. Sally was late, so the teacher kept <u>her</u> inside.

   g. After <u>he</u> finished his homework, Mark went to bed.

   h. <u>She</u> had a blister, but Sally kept on walking.

2. **Choose the correct pronoun from the box to write in each space in the story.**

my	it	you	She	he	her

   One day Mike was walking along the street when _____

   saw Sally. _____ was carrying a puppy in _____

   arms. "What are _____ doing with that puppy?" asked

   Mike. "I am taking _____ to school to show _____

   classmates," she replied.

Pronouns

Pronouns are words that take the places of nouns. Some pronouns tell us that something belongs to someone. Take this example: John kicked *his* ball. The possessive pronoun *his* tells us that the ball belongs to John.

Write the correct pronoun in each space.

a. The dog belongs to Mary.
   The dog is _____. (hers his)

b. The car belongs to Mr. Smith.
   The car is _____. (him his)

c. This ball belongs to me.
   This ball is _____. (its mine)

d. The ball belongs to you.
   The ball is _____. (yours his)

e. These bikes belong to us.
   These bikes are _____. (yours ours)

Conjunctions

Introduction

Conjunctions are words that are used to **join** words or groups of words, including whole sentences. First and second grade students can refer to them as **joining words**.

Examples: Peter rode his bike. John rode his bike.
Peter *and* John rode their bikes.
We did not come. We were ill.
We did not come *because* we were ill.

Children should be made familiar with the following conjunctions through informal discussions and class activities.

if	*but*	*though*	*unless*	*which*
as	*yet*	*until*	*whether*	*who*
and	*when*	*while*	*because*	*or*
for	*that*	*since*	*although*	*also*

Teaching Strategies

Glue for two

Tear a piece of paper in two and show children how it can be joined with glue or sticky tape. Now write two sentences on the board. Show children how these can be joined also, but this time instead of glue or sticky tape, we use a comma and a conjunction.

I washed the dishes. Sally dried them.
I washed the dishes, and Sally dried them.
You must hurry. You will miss the train.
You must hurry, or you will miss the train.

Provide children with numerous simple and informal exercises, having them suggest words suitable to join the sentences.

After the join

Have children orally finish sentences you have written on the chalkboard.

We laughed when . . .
I have not seen him since . . .
I was scared because . . .
We were afraid when . . .
I will not help you unless . . .

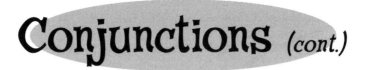

Conjunctions *(cont.)*

Use the conjunction

Provide children with exercises in which they use a given conjunction to join pairs of sentences.

Use a comma and *but*.

Mike is tall. Tom is short.   *Mike is tall, but Tom is short.*
A fire is hot. Ice is cold.   *A fire is hot, but ice is cold.*
I am tired. I can walk.   *I am tired, but I can walk.*

Choose the conjunction

Provide a list of conjunctions on the chalkboard and have children finish sentences by using each one.

because, and, before, until

I cleaned my teeth _____ I went to bed.
We did not go _____ it was raining.
Tom grabbed the apple _____ ate it.
Jane did not leave _____ she was through.

Conjunction search

Conduct a conjunction search from a common text, such as a photocopy of a story or poem already read. Have children read the text and circle any conjunctions they find.

Which conjunction?

Have children orally suggest suitable conjunctions for sentences which you read aloud.

I cannot come. My leg is sore. (if, because)
Their dog was trained. Ours was not trained. (while, but)
Joanne went to bed early. She was very tired. (for, until)
I cannot watch TV. My homework is not done. (because, since)

Conjunctions

Name _____   Grammar BLM **59**

Conjunctions are joining words. They are used to join words and groups of words, including sentences.

1. **Join these sentences using all the words in both sentences, a comma, and the joining word and. Write the new sentence on the line.**

   a. I went into the shop. I bought an ice cream.

   _____

   b. The boy opened the door. He walked in.

   _____

   c. I picked up the glass. I filled it with water.

   _____

   d. Mike saw the jet. Bill saw the jet too.

   _____

2. **Join these sentences by using all the words in both sentences, a comma, and the joining word but.**

   a. An elephant is big. A mouse is tiny.

   _____

   b. The stars are shining. The moon is behind a cloud.

   _____

   c. Feathers are soft. Steel is hard.

   _____

Conjunctions

Conjunctions are joining words. They are used to join words and groups of words, including sentences.

Choose a joining word from the box to write in the space in each sentence.

(because   until   when   before   although   and   if   so)

a. I will buy you an ice cream _____ you finish all the jobs.

b. We did not go swimming _____ the water was too cold.

c. The children began to misbehave _____ our teacher left the room.

d. Sally still played volleyball _____ her leg was sore.

e. I played the piano, _____ Sally played the drums.

f. They went inside _____ it got too hot.

g. We must stay inside _____ the rain stops.

h. Mike set the alarm for seven o'clock _____ he would not be late for school.

Conjunctions

Conjunctions are joining words. They are used to join words and groups of words, including sentences.

1. **Circle the conjunctions. Then complete these sentences in your own words.**

   a. He fell off his bike when

   _____

   b. She was given an ice cream because

   _____

   c. Mike stayed outside while

   _____

   d. She turned on the faucet, and then she

   _____

2. **Now circle the conjunctions and complete these sentences.**

   a. We went for a swim, but we

   _____

   b. The dog bit him because

   _____

   c. She was late for school, and she also

   _____

   d. We put the heater on because

   _____

Conjunctions

Conjunctions are joining words. They are used to join words and groups of words, including sentences.

1. Use all the words in both sentences, a comma, and the joining word **so** to join each pair of sentences.

   a. We were cold. We lit a fire.

   _____

   b. Mary could not do the work. I helped her.

   _____

   c. It began to rain. I hurried.

   _____

   d. The apple was ripe. I ate it.

   _____

   e. The girl was tired. She went to bed.

   _____

2. **Underline the more suitable ending.**

   a. I was hot, so (I lit a fire. I had a cold drink.)

   b. Mike gave me the ball, so (I thanked him. I hit him.)

   c. Mrs. Smith put on her glasses so (she could read the book. she could clap her hands.)

   d. Tom boiled the water so (he could make a hot drink. he could read a book.)

   e. Sally put the saddle on the horse so (she could ride it. she could pick some flowers.)

Sentences

Introduction

A **sentence** is a group of words that makes sense and contains a verb. Take the example *into the box*. This is not a sentence as it does not have a verb and does not make sense by itself. A sentence begins with a capital letter and ends with a period, question mark, or exclamation mark.

There are four types of sentences.

(a) **Statements** simply state something or give information about something.

Examples: *It is hot. The time is eight o'clock. Koalas are marsupials.*

(b) **Questions** ask something.

Examples: *What is the weather like? What time is it? What is a koala?*

(c) **Commands** or **requests** direct someone to do something. They can also give advice or warnings.

Examples: *Get out your books. Sit up. Look out for sharp stones.*

(d) **Exclamations** express the strong feeling of the speaker or writer about something.

Examples: *Ouch! I did it! What a grand day!*

Sentences can take several forms.

(a) **Simple sentences** consist of one clause. They can be divided into two parts: the **subject**, which tells who or what did something, and the **predicate**, which contains the verb and tells us what the subject did or is doing.

Examples: *Horses (subject) run (predicate).*
Billy (subject) climbed the tree (predicate).

Although the terms subject and predicate need not be mentioned at this level, it is important that children do come to see that a sentence tells us who or what did something and what they did.

(b) **Complex sentences** have more than one verb and thus have more than one clause. A complex sentence has at least one **main clause** (independent clause) and one or more **subordinate clauses** (dependent clauses).

Example: *When it was hot we went for a swim because we wanted to get cool.*

(c) **Compound sentences** consist of two or more **main clauses** (independent clauses) joined by a conjunction and, usually, a comma.

Example: *I washed the dishes, and Billy dried them.*

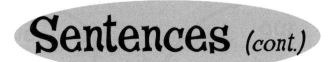

Sentences *(cont.)*

Teaching Strategies

Complete the sentence

Have children add words to complete a sentence. Informal exercises such as this demonstrate to children that a sentence must express a complete thought.

Bill has a new . . . .

I . . . a rabbit.

Answer the question

Ask children questions and have them answer in complete sentences. Children could also be organized in pairs and take turns to ask and answer questions. The game could be made more fun by allowing children to make up silly questions.

What is your name?

My name is Miles Joseph Smith.

Jumbled sentences

Write a series of jumbled sentences on the chalkboard. Challenge children to orally unjumble them.

lives dog a kennel in a

Interview

Choose a volunteer to imagine that he or she has just returned from the moon. Have the rest of the class imagine that they are reporters and ask suitable questions which the moon traveller must answer in complete sentences.

Is the surface of the moon dry?

How long did it take you to get to the moon?

Select other volunteers to take on other roles for the class to question, for example, computer games inventor, Olympic diver, president.

Sentence formulas

Have students compose sentences according to formulas like the ones below. They can also make up their own sentence formulas to exchange with their classmates.

noun	+	verb				
Dogs		*bark.*				
article	+	noun	+	verb		
The		*dogs*		*bark.*		
article	+	adjective	+	noun	+	verb
The		*big*		*dogs*		*bark.*

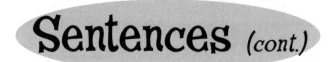

Sentences *(cont.)*

Complete the sentence

Have children complete sentences that you have begun or begin sentences that you have finished. Activities such as this help children understand that sentences have a part that tells who or what did something and a part that tells what they did.

A spider climbed . . .
A dog chased . . .
. . . swam across the creek.
. . . bit the boy on the leg.

Match up

Have children match the beginnings of sentences to the best endings.

The dog   get wool from sheep.
We   climbed the tree.
The monkey barked at the stranger.

Yes or no

Read out statements to the children. Have them answer "yes" or "no."

A puppy is a young cat.
Zebras are black and yellow.

Headline hunt

Have children search through newspapers and cut out the headline words. Have them use the words to create sentences of their own and then paste their sentences onto a sheet of paper.

What am I?

Read a description of an object and ask children to guess what it is. Point out the statements and question in the description, and ask children to answer with a complete sentence. Challenge children to make up their own "What am I?" statements and questions.

I am small. I have wings. I am an insect. I make honey.
What am I?
I am a bee.

Sentences

A sentence must make sense and must contain a subject and a verb.

1. **Circle the sentence in each pair and give it the correct end punctuation.**

   a. My father a joke
      My father told me a joke

   b. The gray horse pulled the cart
      Pulled the cart

   c. I have a
      I have a pet mouse

   d. Her new jumper to school
      Sally wore her new jumper to school

2. **Add words of your own to make sentences. Be sure to use end punctuation and capital letters. The first one has been done for you.**

   a. dog   chewed   bone
      A hungry dog eagerly chewed a juicy bone.

   b. boy   lost   dollar
      _____

   c. truck   crashed   fence
      _____

   d. puppy   dug   hole   garden
      _____

Sentences

Sentences have a part that tells who or what did something and a part that tells what they did.

1. **Put the words in the correct order to make a sentence. Capitalize and punctuate.**

   a. elephants   strong   are

   _____

   b. fly   birds   can

   _____

   c. cake   a   baked   Sandy

   _____

   d. shoelaces   can   I   tie   my

   _____

2. **Draw lines to match each beginning to its correct ending.**

   a. The dog began to quack.

   b. A car   has a hump.

   c. A flower has four legs.

   d. The cookhas a large trunk.

   e. The duckbarked at the stranger.

   f. The elephant made some cakes.

   g. A camel has an engine.

   h. A table has petals.

Sentences

A sentence must make sense and must contain a subject and a verb.

1. **Circle the best words to complete each sentence.**

   a. Every house has (a door   a dog   one flower).

   b. We use crayons (to play with   to draw   to eat).

   c. A horse has four (eyes   legs   ears).

   d. A clock tells us (our age   the weather   the time).

   e. Clowns perform in (the circus   church   school).

2. **Add an ending of your own to complete each sentence.**

   a. A kangaroo has two _____.

   b. A giant is very _____.

   c. A dentist cares for our _____.

   d. Most birds can _____.

   e. Pencils are used for _____.

Sentences

A sentence must make sense and must contain a subject and a verb.

1. **Circle the endings that would make sentences.**

   a. The teacher   some white chalk.
                         told us to stand.
                         read us a story.
                         a television.

   b. A large dog   barked at the cat.
                         with four legs.
                         chewed the bone.
                         very savage.

   c. The small bird   built a nest in the tree.
                         on the lawn.
                         is singing a song.
                         black feathers.

   d. The train   very big.
                         stopped at the station.
                         on the tracks.
                         carried over sixty people

2. **Add a verb of your own and end punctuation to make a proper sentence.**

   I in the puddle

Sentences

Simple sentences are made up of one clause. They contain a subject and a verb, and they make sense on their own.

1. **Add a subject from the box to complete each simple sentence.**

   > The dog   A fish   The car   My bicycle

   a. _____ can swim.

   b. _____ had a flat tire.

   c. _____ is red.

   d. _____ barked.

2. **Beside each picture, write a simple sentence to tell what each person is doing.**

   a.

   _____

   b.

   _____

   c.

   _____

   d.

   _____

Sentences

A compound sentence is made up of two or more main clauses joined by a conjunction (joining word).

Circle the ending that best completes each compound sentence.

a. Mike is going to the dentist   because his toe hurts.
    because he has a toothache.
    because he is thirsty.

b. Sally was feeling tired   because she had eaten some lollipops.
    because she had slept all day.
    because she went to bed late.

c. Tom can't ride to school   because he is twenty years old.
    because his bike is broken.
    because it is a sunny day.

d. Tammy was crying   because she was feeling unhappy.
    because she was feeling happy.
    because she was eating lollipops.

e. Mom filled the gas tank   because it was nearly empty.
    because the car has four wheels.
    because the car has rubber tires.

Prepositional Phrases

Introduction

A phrase is made up of several words but does not contain a subject-verb combination. Usually a phrase functions in a sentence as an adjective or an adverb but sometimes as a noun. Phrases are used to add meaning and interest to sentences. The most common type of phrase is the **prepositional phrase**. It can function in a sentence as an adjective, an adverb, or a noun.

(a) **Adjective**

The girl *with long hair* is coming to the party. (The prepositional phrase *with long hair* is an adjective phrase modifying the subject of the sentence—the noun "girl.")

(b) **Adverb**

The boy kicked the ball *with a lot of skill*. (The prepositional phrase *with a lot of skill* is an adverb phrase modifying the verb of the sentence—"kicked.")

(c) **Noun**

Beneath the bridge is the trolls' home. (The prepositional phrase *Beneath the bridge* is a noun phrase functioning as the subject of the sentence.)

Teaching Strategies

Add a preposition

Have children add a suitable preposition to begin a phrase.

The cow jumped _____ the moon.
The cow jumped over the moon.
Yesterday he went _____ the mountains.
Yesterday he went to the mountains.
We walked _____ the crowded street.
We walked down the crowded street.
Josephine saw a bull _____ the field.
Josephine saw a bull in the field.
Rob would not go _____ the new dog.
Rob would not go near the new dog.
Louise could not see _____ the wall.
Louise could not see over the wall.
Astrid left _____ the bell rang.
Astrid left before the bell rang.

Prepositional Phrases *(cont.)*

Stick-figure phrases

Draw simple stick figures to illustrate the position of a person, animal, or object. Have children say the position each is in.

The cat is *under the table.*

The cat is *on the table.*

Classroom phrases

Have children indicate the positions of certain objects in the classroom.

Teacher: Tom, where is the television?

Tom: It is near the table.

Circle the phrases

As children become more confident, have them search through sentences you have prepared, or through a photocopy of a familiar story, and find and circle the prepositional phrases.

Suggest a phrase

Have children suggest adverbial or adjectival prepositional phrases to complete sentences.

The school bell rings *at nine o'clock.*

I saw the girl *with red hair.*

Complete the sentence

Provide plenty of short exercises in which children must select the more suitable prepositional phrase to add to a sentence.

The girl swam	*in the pool.* *on the roof.*
The young lady ate dinner	*off the plate.* *under the floor.*
Johnny galloped	*through the door.* *above the sky.*
Helen went shopping	*at the barn.* *at the mall.*
Larry wore a hat	*with a feather.* *into the bathtub.*

Prepositional Phrases

Name _____   Grammar BLM **69**

A prepositional phrase is a group of words that has no subject and no verb and begins with a preposition.

Add a phrase from the box to complete each sentence.

at Easter	in the nest	in December
in its kennel	with the surfboard	in the kettle

a. The egg is _____ .

b. The dog is _____ .

c. I saw the boy _____ .

d. Christmas is _____ .

e. I boiled the water _____ .

f . We eat chocolate eggs _____ .

Prepositional Phrases

Name _____ Grammar BLM **70**

Some prepositional phrases do the work of an adverb. They tell *how*, *when*, or *where* an action happens.

Look at each underlined phrase. Write *how* if it tells us how an action happens, *when* if it tells us when an action happens, or *where* if it tells us where an action happens.

a. The baby is <u>in the baby carriage</u>. _____

b. We sleep <u>in a bed</u>. _____

c. I cleaned my teeth <u>after lunch</u>. _____

d. Jack's balloon burst <u>with a loud bang</u>. _____

e. There is a television <u>in the room</u>. _____

f. We finished <u>before playtime</u>. _____

g. I go to bed <u>in the evening</u>. _____

h. I climbed <u>up the tree</u>. _____

i. The dogs barked <u>in a noisy manner</u>. _____

j. The man spoke <u>in an angry voice</u>. _____

Prepositional Phrases

Some prepositional phrases do the work of an adverb. They tell *how*, *when*, or *where* an action happens.

Choose the best phrase to tell where each action is happening.

under the tree	in the oven	on the table
in the park	on the rug	to Sally
across the playground		into the jug

a. The drinking glasses are _____ .

b. I poured the milk _____ .

c. We played football _____ .

d. Dad cooked a chicken _____ .

e. Jimmy threw the ball _____ .

f. We ran _____ .

g. Mushrooms are growing _____ .

h. The dog fell asleep _____ .

Prepositional Phrases

Some prepositional phrases do the work of an adverb. They tell *how*, *when*, or *where* an action happens.

Choose the best phrase to tell when each action is happening.

at nine o'clock	at four o'clock	at six o'clock
at eleven o'clock	at eight o'clock	at midnight

a. The school day ends _____.

b. I caught the train _____.

c. I went to bed _____.

d. I ate some lunch _____.

e. I ate my breakfast _____.

f. Dad went to bed _____.

Prepositional Phrases

Name _____   Grammar BLM **73**

Some prepositional phrases do the work of an adverb. They tell *how*, *when*, or *where* an action happens.

Choose the best phrase to tell how each action is happening.

> in silence   with a single blow   in a noisy way
> without fear   at great speed   in a friendly manner

a. He broke the glass

_____ .

b. The teacher spoke to me

_____ .

c. We ate our meal

_____ .

d. The car raced along the street

_____ .

e. The dogs yelped

_____ .

f. The brave girl ran into the blazing house

_____ .

Prepositional Phrases

Name _____ Grammar BLM **74**

Prepositional phrases add meaning and interest to sentences. In a sentence, the phrase should be placed close to the word it helps or describes.

Rewrite each sentence, placing the underlined prepositional phrase in the correct place.

a. The boy built a sandcastle <u>with blue swim trunks</u>.

_____

b. The girl ate an ice-cream cone <u>with glasses</u>.

_____

c. The horse kicked the man <u>with a long tail</u>.

_____

d. The old man sat on the seat <u>with a long, gray beard</u>.

_____

e. The rabbit dived into the burrow <u>with a fluffy tail</u>.

_____

f. The lady killed a snake <u>with sunscreen on her face</u>.

_____

Prepositional Phrases

A prepositional phrase is a group of words that has no subject or verb and begins with a preposition.

1. **Circle the phrase that better completes each sentence.**

   a. I saw the rabbit (with fluffy ears   with large horns).

   b. I picked the flower (with big ears   with lots of petals).

   c. We played football (on the field   in the classroom).

   d. We went for a picnic (in the streetcar   in the park).

2. **Prepositional phrases begin with a preposition. Write phrases beginning with each of the prepositions below.**

   a. under _____

   b. on _____

   c. with _____

   d. in _____

   e. near _____

   f. beside _____

Clauses

Introduction

A **clause** is a group of words that contains a verb and its subject. First and second grade students can think of clauses as groups of words that tell about an action.

There are two types of clauses.

(a) A **main clause** (independent clause) contains the main thought of the sentence and makes sense standing alone.

> Examples: *I spoke to the teacher* who is our football coach.
> *The dog* that was barking *chased me across the lawn.*

(b) A **subordinate clause** (dependent clause) cannot make sense standing on its own. To make a sentence, a subordinate clause must be added to a main clause.

> Examples: I saw the dog *when I came home.*
> They went to the shop *so they could buy ice cream.*

Subordinate clauses add information to a sentence and function in the same ways as **adjectives, adverbs,** or **nouns**.

> Examples: That's the house *where Susan lives.* (adjective)
> She visited *where Susan lives.* (adverb)
> I don't know *where Susan lives.* (noun)

Teaching Strategies

The main thing

Provide students with practice in finding the main clause in a sentence by having them search through a photocopy of a familiar story, circling the main clauses. Remind them that a main clause can stand alone and contains the main thought of the sentence. Point out that a simple sentence is, in fact, one main clause.

Main clause beep

Have children sit in a circle. Choose a child to say a word to start a clause. Each child in turn then adds a word to build a main clause. When the clause is complete, the next child says "Beep." The game can be extended to add a subordinate clause to the main clause.

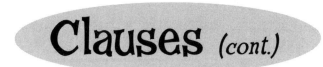
Clauses (cont.)

Act the clause
Organize children in groups of four. Tell groups that the first child is to provide a verb, the second child is to provide a subject, the third child is to arrange the verb and subject to make a clause, and the fourth child is to act out the clause. Ensure that all children get a turn in each role.

Clause match-up
Have children match main clauses to subordinate clauses. This is also an excellent reading activity.

These are the brave boys   *because he was feeling ill.*
Bill did not come   *where the bus stop was.*
The bus driver didn't know   *who rescued the drowning child.*

Clause call-out
Write a main clause on the chalkboard and challenge children to call out appropriate subordinate clauses.

We went to the park   *after we had eaten lunch.*
                          where the willow tree grows.
                          because we wanted to play.

Make connections
Subordinate conjunctions are the words used to introduce subordinate clauses. They are the words that connect the subordinate clause to the main clause. Have students choose from a list of subordinate conjunctions to connect main clauses to subordinate clauses.

subordinate conjunctions
unless
if
while
before
until

Billy said he would not go _____ *Jeremy was going to be there.*

His mother said he could play outside _____ *it was dinnertime.*

Jack watched the zoo animals _____ *he was waiting for Margo.*

Father will go to the meeting _____ *he has the time.*

I got to the meeting _____ *he got there.*

Clauses

A clause is a group of words that tells about an action. A main clause contains the main thought of the sentence and makes sense standing alone.

1. **Circle the main clause in each sentence.**

   a. This is the dog that stole the sausages.

   b. I spoke to the boy who climbed the tree.

   c. I found the ring that the lady had lost.

   d. I helped the girl who had broken her leg.

   e. This is the cow which had twin calves.

   f. The teacher growled at the boy who is always talking.

   g. This is the house where Katy lives.

   h. The bird flew away when the bell rang.

2. **Choose two of the sentences above. Rewrite each one with a new main clause.**

   a. _____

   _____

   b. _____

   _____

Clauses

A clause is a group of words that tells about an action. A main clause contains the main thought of the sentence and makes sense standing alone.

1. **Here are some main clauses. Add a subordinate clause to each one to make longer sentences.**

   a. There is the clown _____ .

   b. This is the house _____ .

   c. There goes the cat _____ .

   d. I climbed the tree _____ .

   e. This is the girl _____ .

2. **Add a main clause to complete each sentence.**

   a. _____ when he fell.

   b. _____ that had fallen.

   c. _____ when the bell rings.

   d. _____ who plays football.

   e. _____ which bit my mother.

Clauses

A compound sentence has two main clauses joined by a conjunction (joining word) and usually has a comma before the conjunction. Each of these clauses has its own subject and verb.

1. **Circle the joining word. Underline each clause.**

   a. The child hit the puppy, and it ran away.

   b. My leg feels sore, and my foot is bleeding.

   c. I want you to finish the work, or I will not help you.

   d. Get that work done, or the teacher will keep you in.

   e. I washed the dishes, and Sally dried them.

   f. We must leave now, or we will get wet.

   g. I did not win the race, but I did not come in last.

   h. Cows give us milk, and sheep give us wool.

2. **Write two compound sentences of your own.**

   a. _____

   _____

   b. _____

   _____

Punctuation

Introduction

The fundamentals of **punctuation** are best introduced to students when they are in the first and second grades. The main elements that need to be taught are as follows.

A **capital letter** is used for
(a) the first letter of a sentence
(b) the first letter of a person's given name and family name
(c) the pronoun *I*
(d) the first letter of names of the days of the week, months of the year, and special times such as *Easter, Christmas*
(e) the first letter of names of towns, cities, countries, streets, schools, etc.

A **period** is used at the end of a statement or command sentence.
Examples: *That dog is brown.* (statement)
Sit down. (command)

A **question mark** is used at the end of a sentence that is a direct question. It might be helpful to point out the question indicators *who, when, where, why, what,* and *how.*
Examples: *What is the time?* (direct question)
I asked her what the time was. (indirect question)

An **exclamation point** is used at the end of a sentence that expresses a strong emotion. Point out to children that exclamations are often short.
Examples: *Wow!   Ouch!   Well done!*

Commas are used to separate words in a list.
Examples: *Please go to the store and buy oranges, bread, milk, and butter.* (separate nouns)
It was a big, black, hairy spider. (separate adjectives)
Please work quickly, neatly, and quietly. (separate adverbs)

Quotation marks are used to enclose the words actually spoken by someone. Children in the first and second grades can call them talking marks.
Examples: *Ali asked, "When are we going?"*
"Let's go now," said Ben.

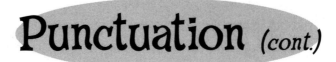
Punctuation *(cont.)*

Teaching Strategies

Don't pause for breath

Begin reading a story to the children but do not pause at any punctuation marks. The children will be confused and will object to the speed of your reading. As soon as this happens, lead them into an informal discussion on the need for punctuation marks when we write.

Beep marks

Read a simple story aloud to the children. Whenever you reach a punctuation mark, say "Beep!" The children must then supply the missing mark.

Body sculptures

Have children work in groups to use their bodies to make punctuation marks such as an exclamation mark (one body lying stretched out with another curled in a ball at its feet), a period (all huddled in together), a proper noun (first letter standing tall for a capital and others on knees for small letters), and so on.

Model marks

Allow children to explore different punctuation marks by making them in clay or other 3-D materials.

Do the sentence stamp

Read a simple story aloud to the children. Have children listen carefully for the different punctuation marks and perform the following actions at the appropriate moments:

capital letter	*Put your hand up.*
period	*Clap your hands.*
exclamation mark	*Stamp your feet.*
question mark	*Jump up.*

Question or statement?

Write a sentence on the chalkboard. Have the children determine whether it is a question or a statement and punctuate it accordingly.

Punctuation search

Have the children search through old magazines and newspapers, cutting out capital letters and other punctuation marks that appear in large print. Children can then paste the punctuation marks on a sheet of paper headed "My Punctuation Marks Sheet."

Punctuation

A capital letter is used for
- **the first letter of a sentence**
- **the first letter of a person's name**
- **the pronoun *I***
- **the first letter of names of the days of the week, months of the year, and special times such as Easter, Christmas**
- **the first letter of names of towns, cities, countries, streets, and so on.**

1. **Circle the words that should begin with a capital letter.**

horse	elephant	table
christmas	samuel	judy
monday	teacher	pen
sunday	john	easter
april	bucket	cup
megan	tuesday	december
chicago	day	key

2. **Rewrite the sentences, using correct punctuation.**

a. the old man rode his bicycle to the town of sea lake

_____

b. i saw sam and joanne in wattle street

_____

c. we are leaving next monday morning

_____

Punctuation

Name _____   Grammar BLM **80**

A statement sentence ends with a period.
A question sentence ends with a question mark.

1. Add a word to each line to make a question. Don't forget to punctuate correctly.

    a. where you live _____

    b. what your name _____

    c. you like pizza _____

2. In each line there are two sentences. One is a statement, and one is a question. Rewrite both, putting in the correct punctuation marks and capital letters.

    a. do you think john will come he should be here now

    _____

    _____

    b. where is the cat i haven't seen it all day

    _____

    _____

    c. the clouds are getting dark do you think it will rain

    _____

    _____

Punctuation

A comma is used to separate words in a list.

1. Add the commas.

   a. I ate peas chips and bread for lunch.

   b. On our farm we have pigs cows and horses.

   c. All trees have leaves bark and roots.

   d. At school I play volleyball football tennis and softball.

2. Add a list to complete each sentence.

   a. My best friends are _____

   _____

   b. My favorite foods are _____

   _____

   c. My favorite animals are _____

   _____

Punctuation

Name _____   Grammar BLM **82**

An exclamation point is used at the end of a sentence that expresses a strong emotion. Exclamation sentences are often short.

1. **Add an exclamation mark in the box after each of these.**

   a. Wow ☐   f. Thief ☐

   b. Ouch ☐   g. What a lovely puppy ☐

   c. Look out ☐   h. Yuck ☐

   d. Eek ☐   i. How terrible ☐

   e. Stop ☐

2. **What might you call out if the following happened? Write an exclamation for each situation.**

   a. You stick a pin in your finger.

   _____

   b. You win a race after training very hard.

   _____

   c. You drop your ice cream.

   _____

Punctuation

Quotation marks (talking marks) are used around the exact words that someone says.
"I like football," said Tom.
Tom said, "I like football."

1. Add the quotation marks.

a. I saw Peter, said Mary.

b. We hate getting up early, said the boys.

c. Sam yelled, Where did Tom find it?

d. My best friend said, I will help you.

e. Betty, come here, cried Mavis.

2. Add words of your own inside the quotation marks.

a. "_____," cried the baby.

b. "_____," said the teacher.

c. My mother asked, "_____?"

d. Sally yelled, "_____!"

e. "_____," laughed Toby.

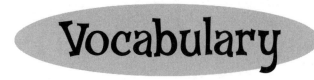

Introduction

Grammar is also concerned with the way an overall sentence or composition is structured to engage an audience and to deliver its message, including the way we choose particular words appropriate to that audience and message. It is important to generate an interest in words and to encourage children to be thoughtful about the words they use. If children develop an interest in language at an early age, they should continue throughout their school lives and into adulthood appreciating the richness and diversity of our ever-growing language.

Teaching Strategies

Add a word

Use every opportunity to interest children in words. Informal exercises are suitable for this. Have children add words orally to a sentence that you begin.

Tom is big, but Sam is . . .

Describing words

Challenge children to think of as many words as possible to describe an object or person.

apple: red, juicy, crunchy, rotten, smelly

Homophone hunt

Write a list of words on the chalkboard. Challenge children to think of the corresponding homophones. Children can also create cartoons to illustrate the homophones.

allowed/aloud	*ate/eight*	*eye/I*
bare/bear	*bean/been*	*blew/blue*
board/bored	*brake/break*	*flea/flee*
hear/here	*knit/nit*	*one/won*
pair/pear	*sun/son*	

Sort the words

Supply children with numerous words written on small cardboard squares. Have children classify the words into categories.

animals:	*cow*	*dog*	*cat*
birds:	*crow*	*dove*	*sparrow*

Vocabulary (cont.)

Fish

On blank playing cards write pairs of synonyms, antonyms, or homophones. Encourage children to play "Go fish!" with them.

Scattered letters

Write a selection of letters scattered on the chalkboard. Have children think of as many words as they can using the letters. Make the game more challenging by introducing a timer.

Word collection

Organize a word-collection bulletin board in the classroom. Encourage children to find, collect, and then display words on the board. The board could have a number of different headings, such as Interesting Words, Words That Sound Funny, Words That Sound Like Noises, Words That Sound Important. Ask children to think of other headings they would like to use.

Tongue twisters

Challenge children to say a tongue twister quickly. Then have them make up their own tongue twisters for their friends to try.

She sells seashells by the seashore.

Word partners

Have students supply both a *synonym* and an *antonym* for commonly used words such as these.

lovely
cool
funny
awful
terrible
crazy
cute
sweet

Opposites

Find a word in the grid to complete each sentence.

d	l	a	t	e
r	s	t	o	p
y	l	o	n	g
b	w	e	s	t
o	l	e	f	t
y	l	o	s	e

a. I wanted to go, but Mom said to _____.

b. My string is short, but yours is _____.

c. I think he will win, and I might _____.

d. My hair is wet, but yours is _____.

e. Sam came early, but Kathy was _____.

f. Sally is a girl, but Mike is a _____.

g. I went east, but she went _____.

h. This is my right arm, and this is my _____ arm.

Synonyms

1. **One word in each line has a similar meaning to the word in the first column. Color that box.**

rock	cow	ice	table	stone
sick	ill	silly	old	blue
rug	bug	horse	mat	book
fast	slow	quick	big	pretty
little	small	tired	sea	damp
chair	car	bike	seat	tree
tidy	cold	neat	under	bowl

2. **Use from the box a word that has a similar meaning to replace the underlined word.**

fix	start	glad	nap

a. We waited for the game to <u>begin</u>.

   _____

b. I helped my mother <u>mend</u> the broken glass.

   _____

c. I had a short <u>sleep</u>.

   _____

d. I am <u>happy</u> that you could come.

   _____

Word Families

Name _____ Grammar BLM **86**

1. **Color the box that contains the word that does not belong with the others in the row.**

apple	banana	dog	grape	pear
table	pencil	pen	crayon	chalk
roof	door	window	wall	train
pie	flower	cake	ice cream	pudding
wolf	dog	fox	coyote	bus
chair	book	seat	stool	sofa
face	arms	legs	neck	street
cup	coat	shirt	sweater	socks

2. **Write the word that does not belong in each group.**

a. tree lion bush shrub _____

b. start begin go shop _____

c. cheese salt cream milk _____

d. sun star moon bed _____

e. rake chair spade shovel _____

f. sheet blanket grass pillow _____

Word Families

Name _____ Grammar BLM **87**

1. **Sort the words in the box and write them under the headings.**

yellow	sweater	shoes	softball	football	red
golf	tie	socks	hockey	green	blue

Sports	Colors	Clothing
_____	_____	_____
_____	_____	_____
_____	_____	_____
_____	_____	_____

2. **Choose from the box and write on the line the word that says what the things in the row are.**

animals flowers insects colors drinks vegetables

a. tea coffee milk lemonade _____

b. blue red yellow green _____

c. wolf dog cat zebra _____

d. rose violet daisy daffodil _____

e. carrot lettuce onion potato _____

f. fly wasp beetle ant _____

Compound Words

1. **Add a word from the box to complete each compound word.**

book	pot	berry	dog	fish	mill

a. straw _____

b. tea _____

c. note _____

d. wind _____

e. star _____

f. bull _____

2. **Use the words in the box to make a name to write beside each picture.**

tooth	pop	light	brush	corn	house

a. _____

b. _____

c. _____

Anagrams

An anagram is a word made by rearranging all the letters of another word.

Rearrange the letters of each word to make a word to match the picture.

a. nap _____

b. tar _____

c. pat _____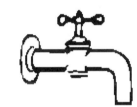

d. ram _____

e. pot _____

f. slip _____

Similes

Name _____   Grammar BLM **90**

A simile is a group of words that compares one thing to another by using the words *like* or *as*.

1. Use the words in the box to complete the similes.

as light as a	as slow as a	as hot as
as cold as	as busy as a	as wise as an

a. _____ bee

b. _____ snail

c. _____ feather

d. _____ fire

e.  _____ owl

f. _____ ice

2. Add a word of your own to complete each simile.

a. as green as

b. as big as _____

c. as flat as _____

d. as strong as

Word Fun

1. Add one letter to make a word that matches the picture.

a.   _____ all

b.   _____ our

c. 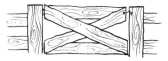   _____ ate

d.   _____ oat

e.   _____ ar

2. Drop one letter to make a word that matches the picture. Write the word on the line.

a.   bone _____

b.    farm _____

c.   pear _____

d.    clock _____

e.    nest _____

Review

Name _____   Grammar BLM **92**

1. **On the lines below, write words that can be used as the parts of speech listed.**

   a. one noun _____

   b. two verbs _____ _____

   c. three adjectives _____ _____ _____

   d. two adverbs _____ _____

   e. one article _____

   f. one prepositional phrase (preposition + article + noun)

   _____

   g. one pronoun _____

   h. one conjunction _____

2. **Write one sentence using as many as you can of the words you wrote on the lines above. You may put them in any order you choose, and you may add conjunctions, commas, and articles.**

   (You might end up with a sentence as silly as this one: Beautiful and bold, Betsy slowly strolled and silently skipped through the tulips.)

   _____

   _____

   _____

   _____

   _____

Review

1. Write two examples for each of the following kinds of nouns.

a. singular noun

_____   _____

b. plural noun

_____   _____

c. common noun

_____   _____

d. proper noun

_____   _____

e. collective noun

_____   _____

2. Write two examples for each of the following verb tenses.

a. present tense

_____   _____

b. past tense

_____   _____

c. future tense

_____   _____

Review

1. Write two adjectives to describe each of the following nouns.

a. penguin

_____   _____

b. classmates

_____   _____

c. toolbox

_____   _____

d. Abraham Lincoln

_____   _____

e. herd

_____   _____

2. Write two adverbs to describe each of the following past tense verbs.

a. dived   _____   _____

b. shook   _____   _____

c. flowed   _____   _____

d. said   _____   _____

e. wrote   _____   _____

Review

1. **List two prepositions that could be used with each of the following groups of words.**

   a. _____ _____ the sofa

   b. _____ _____ the street

   c. _____ _____ the sea

   d. _____ _____ the soil

   e. _____ _____ the sun

   f. _____ _____ the scalp

   g. _____ _____ the statue

2. **List two pronouns that could be used to indicate who owns each of the listed objects. (Use each pronoun only once.)**

   a. _____ _____ purple pencil

   b. _____ _____ pet porcupine

   c. _____ _____ paper plane

   d. _____ _____ poor partner

   e. _____ _____ powerful pirate

   f. _____ _____ party plans

   g. _____ _____ pretty pal

Review

1. On the line after the sentence, label the sentence *question*, *statement*, *exclamation*, or *command*.

    a. Once upon a time a student was studying grammar.

      _____

    b. "Why do I have to know this stuff?"

      _____

    c. "Do you speak English?"

      _____

    d. "Yes!"

      _____

    e. "That answers your question."

      _____

2. Write two simple sentences.

    a. _____

    b. _____

3. Write one compound sentence.

    _____

    _____

Review

1. **On the lines below, write one synonym (same) and one antonym (opposite) for each word.**

    a. good   _____   _____

    b. wonderful _____   _____

    c. happy   _____   _____

    d. sad   _____   _____

    e. bad   _____   _____

2. **Write a simile to describe the following actions and feelings. Use one you have heard or read or make up your own simile.**

    a. Alma is very happy.

    _____

    b. Bob is running very fast.

    _____

    c. Clara is walking very slowly.

    _____

    d. Don is very poor today.

    _____

    e. Eliza is very busy today.

    _____

Answer Key

page 12

clockwise   fish

cat   tail

nose   bowl

water   leg

bubble   whisker

fin   eye

page 13

clockwise   eye

dog   leg

tongue   back

mouth   ear

paw

page 14

a. camel

b. mouse

c. giraffe

d. tiger

e. zebra

f. horse

page 15

colored boxes

   column l

     window

     train

     car

   column 2

     bus

   column 3

     flower

     bicycle

page 16

1. *farm animals/red*

   cat

   duck

   ram

   horse

cow

pig

zoo animals/blue

monkey

tiger

giraffe

elephant

zebra

2. *colored boxes*

   column 1

     bird

     table

   column 2

     girl

     man

   column 3

     tiger

     bug

     chair

page 17

a. cow   c. egg

b. star   d. car

page 18

   column 1

     book

     tent

     baby

     duck

   column 2

     box

     ship

     ring

     cow

page 19

a. ant

b. star

c. apple

d. eagle

e. shovel

f. lamb

g. sofa

h. mother

page 20

a. Joanne

b. Tuesday

c. December

d. Spot

e. Terry

f. New York City

page 21

a. Monday

b. Wednesday

c. Thursday

d. Sunday

e. Saturday

   Sunday

page 22

a. swarm

b. flock

c. bunch

d. herd

e. fleet

f. team

g. litter

h. forest

page 23

a. cows   f. trees

b. books   g. cat

c. dogs   h. flower

d. chairs   i. horse

e. rings

page 24

a. children

b. man

c. geese

d. feet

e. tooth

f. women

page 29

column 1

   hop

   row

   sleep

   fly

column 2

   run

   ride

   dance

   fish

page 30

a. fish   e. horse

b. duck   f. clock

c. boat   g. dog

d. rain

page 31

a. kick, ball

b. read, book

c. boil, eggs

d. wear, coat

e. build, sandcastle

f. cut, bread

page 32

Noun

a. sun

b. fish

c. wind

d. duck

e. rain

f. horse

Answer Key (cont.)

page 32 (cont.)

Verb

a. shines
b. swims
c. blows
d. quacks
e. falls
f. trots

page 33

h	b	a	r	k
o	f	l	y	r
p	c	r	y	i
s	w	i	m	n
t	i	c	k	g

a. fly   e. swim
b. bark   f. ring
c. hop   g. tick
d. cry

page 34

1. *Noun–Verbs*
    boy–skip, eat, kick
    snake–slither, bite, hiss
    chicken–drink, eat, scratch
    fish–swim, eat, grow
    dog–eat, bark, play
    horse–gallop, grow, eat
    duck–swim, fly, quack
    fire–burn, heat, cook
    wheel–spin, turn, roll
2. Answers will vary.
3. Answers will vary.

page 35

(Answers will vary.)
    a. sitting

b. throwing
c. standing
d. falls
e. flies
f. growling

s	w	a	m	l
w	a	t	e	i
a	c	r	y	c
s	s	a	w	k
h	h	o	p	e
t	o	l	d	d

page 36

a. told
b. cry
c. saw
d. swam
e. licked
f. wash
g. hop
h. ate

page 37

ate   went
washed   watch
brushed said
put   jumped

page 38

o	p	e	n	e
b	a	k	e	a
t	e	l	l	t
m	a	k	e	s
w	a	s	h	e
p	e	e	l	t

a. wash
b. set
c. bake
d. eat
e. open
f. tell
g. make
h. peel

page 39

Answers will vary.
    a. Lisa kicked the ball.
    b. The dog barked at me.
    c. Our teacher told us a story.
    d. The train arrived at the station.
    e. The puppy chewed the bone.
    f. The kangaroo hopped over the fence.
    g. Sally rang the bell for play.
    h. The bird flew into the tree.

page 40

a. is   f. is
b. are   g. are
c. are   h. is
d. are   i. are
e. is   j. is

page 41

a. was   f. were
b. was   g. were
c. were   h. was
d. was   i. was
e. were   j. were

page 42

1.
    a. ran
    b. sat
    c. jumped
    d. ate
    e. walked
    f. rode
2. Answers will vary.

page 43

1.
    a. like
    b. saw
    c. thought
    d. believed
    e. hated
    f. think
2. Answers will vary.

page 44

1.
    a. hits
    b. barks
    c. sits
    d. sweeps
    e. grow
    f. swims

2.
    a. buys
    b. plants
    c. scratches
    d. jump

page 45

1.
    a. played
    b. broke
    c. ate
    d. dropped
    e. dug
    f. helped

2.
    a. rained
    b. fell
    c. drove
    d. bit

page 46

1.
    a. eat
    b. bite

Answer Key (cont.)

page 46 *(cont.)*
  c. break
  d. come
  e. catch
  f. begin
2.
  a. hide
  b. go
  c. help
  d. win

page 50
  a. yellow
  b. fat
  c. green
  d. round
  e. red
  f. soft
  g. strong
  h. wild
  i. funny
  j. black

page 51
underlined noun/circled adjectives
  a. grass/the, green
  b. flowers/the, red
  c. horse/the, black
  d. house/the, brown
  e. pond/the, blue
  f. ducks/the, yellow

page 52
underlined nouns/ circled adjectives
  a. trees, hill/two, a
  b. bird, tree/a, big, one
  c. tail, bird/a, long, the, big
  d. lizard, tree/a, small, the, second

  e. ant, nose/a, black, the small, lizard's

page 53
  a. big
    small
  b. hot
    cold
  c. high
    low

page 54
1. *noun/adjectives*
  banana/ripe, yellow
  girl/clever, young
  knife/sharp, blunt
  pillow/soft, white
  dress/pretty, dirty
  pig/pink, fat
  door/open, shut
  grass/green, tall
2. *adjectives/yes or no*
  a. A, a, high/no
  b. An, fifteen/no
  c. The, earth's, blue/no
  d. A, dirty, wrinkled/yes

page 55
Answers will vary.
  a. a juicy red apple
  b. a roomy white house
  c. a fat round pencil
  d. a tall oak tree

page 56
1.
  large   ripe
  tiny   tall
  deep   greedy
2. Answers will vary.

  a. a curvy shape
  b. a formal dress
  c. a square table
  d. a sunny day

page 57
1.
  a. white
  b. deep
  c. two
  d. soft
  e. new
2.
  a. tiny
  b. warm
  c. damp
  d. fast
  e. big

page 61
1.
  a. when
  b. how
  c. where
  d. when
  e. how
  f. where
2.
  a. when
  b. when
  c. how
  d. where
  e. where
  f. when
  g. how

page 62
  a. still
  b. early/tonight
  c. softly
  d. there/here
  e. hard

  f. often/tonight
  g. here/there
  h. tonight/often/early

page 63
1.
  a. later
  b. late
  c. there
  d. down
  e. inside
2.
  a. early
  b. quickly
  c. softly
  d. before
  e. now

page 64
Answers will vary.

page 65
  a. strongly
    strong
  b. quickly
    quick
  c. slow
    slowly
  d. sad
    sadly

page 68
1.
  egg   ugly
  axe   ice
  old   emu
  ink   apple
  owl   ox
2.
  a. l   d. z
  b. v   e. i
  c. b   f. o

Answer Key (cont.)

page 69

1.
a. a	g. an
b. an	h. an
c. a	i. a
d. a	j. a
e. an	k. an
f. an	l. an

2.
a. an	e. an
b. a	f. a
c. an	g. an
d. an	h. an

page 70

1.

column 1
orange
ice cream

column 2
umbrella
ant
umpire
arm

column 3
eye
owl
elf
oven

2.
a. an	e. a
b. a	f. an
c. an	g. an
d. a	h. an

page 71

(*across*)
a	an	a
an	an	a
an	a	an
a		

page 72

1. *word/article*
a. snake/the
b. egg/an
c. present/a
d. dog/A
e. bone/the
f. book/a

2.
a. the
b. a/the
c. an/the
d. the
e. an
a. a

page 75
a. above
b. between
c. inside
d. beside
e. under

page 76
a. in
b. under
c. into
d. over
e. behind

page 77
a. with
b. into
c. of
d. from
e. for
f. under
g. by
h. with
i. with
j. by

k. of
l. for

page 78

preposition/better ending
a. on/the lake
b. into/the cold water
c. under/the table
d. down/the stairs
e. of/a tiger
f. in/the forest

page 79

1. *preposition/*
Answers will vary.
a. down
b. into
c. behind
d. above

2.
a. no
b. no
c. no
d. yes

page 82
a. he
b. she
c. it
d. them
e. him
f. her

page 83

1.
a. him
b. I
c. me
d. they
e. her
f. you

2.
his
their
them
him
its
we

page 84

1.
a. Mike
b. Sally
c. dog
d. Megan
e. book
f. Sally
g. Mark
h. Sally

2.
he	you
She	it
her	my

page 85
a. hers
b. his
c. mine
d. yours
e. ours

page 88

1.
a. I went into the shop, and I bought an ice cream.
b. The boy opened the door, and he walked in.
c. I picked up the glass, and I filled it with water.

Answer Key (cont.)

page 88 *(cont.)*

    d. Mike saw the jet, and Bill saw the jet too.

2.

    a. An elephant is big, but a mouse is tiny.

    b. The stars are shining, but the moon is behind a cloud.

    c. Feathers are soft, but steel is hard.

page 89

    a. if

    b. because

    c. when

    d. although

    e. and

    f. before

    g. until

    h. so

page 90

1. *conjunction/ Answers will vary.*

    a. when

    b. because

    c. while

    d. and

2. *conjunction/ Answers will vary.*

    a. but

    b. because

    c. and

    d. because

page 91

1.

    a. We were cold, so we lit a fire.

    b. Mary could not do the work, so I helped her.

    c. It began to rain, so I hurried.

    d. The apple was ripe, so I ate it.

    e. The girl was tired, so she went to bed.

2.

    a. I had a cold drink.

    b. I thanked him.

    c. she could read the book.

    d. he could make a hot drink.

    e. she could ride it.

page 95

1.

    a. My father told me a joke.

    b. The gray horse pulled the cart.

    c. I have a pet mouse.

    d. Sally wore her new jumper to school.

2. Answers will vary.

    a. A hungry dog eagerly chewed a juicy bone.

    b. The unfortunate boy quickly lost his last dollar.

    c. The overloaded truck crashed into the picket fence.

    d. My new puppy dug a big hole in Mother's garden.

page 96

1.

    a. Elephants are strong.

    b. Birds can fly.

    c. Sandy baked a cake.

    d. I can tie my shoelaces.

2.

    a. The dog barked at the stranger.

    b. A car has an engine.

    c. A flower has petals.

    d. The cook made some cakes.

    e. The duck began to quack.

    f. The elephant has a large trunk.

    g. A camel has a hump.

    h. A table has four legs.

page 97

1.

    a. a door

    b. to draw

    c. legs

    d. the time

    e. the circus

2. Answers will vary.

    a. ears/eyes

    b. big/tall

    c. teeth

    d. fly

    e. writing/drawing

page 98

1.

    a. told us to stand. read us a story.

    b. barked at the cat. chewed the bone.

    c. built a nest in the tree. is singing a song.

    d. stopped at the station. carried over sixty people.

2. Answers will vary. I fell in the puddle. *or* I jumped in the puddle.

page 99

1.

    a. A fish

    b. The car

    c. My bicycle

    d. The dog

2. Answers may vary.

    a. She is jumping rope.

    b. He is riding a horse.

    c. He is skateboarding.

    d. He won the race.

page 100

    a. because he has a toothache.

    b. because she went to bed late.

    c. because his bike is broken.

    d. because she was feeling unhappy.

    e. because it was nearly empty.

Answer Key (cont.)

page 103
a. in the nest
b. in its kennel
c. with the surfboard
d. in December
e. in the kettle
f. at Easter

page 104
a. where   f. when
b. where   g. when
c. when   h. where
d. how   i. how
e. where   j. how

page 105
a. on the table
b. into the jug
c. in the park
d. in the oven
e. to Sally
f. across the playground
g. under the tree
h. on the rug

page 106
a. at four o'clock
b. at eight o'clock
c. at nine o'clock
d. at eleven o'clock
e. at six o'clock
f. at midnight

page 107
a. with a single blow
b. in a friendly manner
c. in silence
d. at great speed
e. in a noisy way
f. without fear

page 108
a. The boy with blue swim trunks built a sandcastle.
b. The girl with glasses ate an ice-cream cone.
c. The horse with a long tail kicked the man.
d. The old man with a long, gray beard sat on the seat.
e. The rabbit with a fluffy tail dived into the burrow.
f. The lady with sunscreen on her face killed a snake.

page 109
1.
a. with fluffy ears
b. with lots of petals
c. on the field
d. in the park
2. Answers will vary.

page 112
1.
a. This is the dog
b. I spoke to the boy
c. I found the ring
d. I helped the girl
e. This is the cow
f. The teacher growled at the boy
g. This is the house
h. The bird flew away
2. Answers will vary.

page 113
1. Answers will vary.
2. Answers will vary.

page 114
1. *joining word/ clause/clause*
a. and/The child hit the puppy/it ran away
b. and/My leg feels sore/my foot is bleeding
c. or/I want you to finish the work/I will not help you
d. or/Get that work done/the teacher will keep you in
e. and/I washed the dishes/Sally dried them
f. or/We must leave now/we will get wet
g. but/I did not win the race/I did not come in last
h. and/Cows give us milk/sheep give us wool
2. Answers will vary.

page 117
1.
column 1
Christmas
Monday
Sunday
April
Megan
Chicago
column 2

Samuel
John
Tuesday
column 3
Judy
Easter
December

2.
a. The old man rode his bicycle to the town of Sea Lake.
b. I saw Sam and Joanne in Wattle Street.
c. We are leaving next Monday morning.

page 118
1. Answers will vary.
a. Where do you live?
b. What is your name?
c. Do you like pizza?

2.
a. Do you think John will come? He should be here now.
b. Where is the cat? I haven't seen it all day.
c. The clouds are getting dark. Do you think it will rain?

page 119
1.
a. I ate peas, chips, and bread for lunch.

Answer Key (cont.)

page 119 (cont.)

b. On our farm we have pigs, cows, and horses.

c. All trees have leaves, bark, and roots.

d. At school I play volleyball, football, tennis, and softball.

2. Answers will vary.

page 120

1. Place an exclamation mark in each box.

2. Answers will vary.

page 121

1.

a. "I saw Peter," said Mary.

b. "We hate getting up early," said the boys.

c. Sam yelled, "Where did Tom find it?"

d. My best friend said, "I will help you."

e. "Betty, come here," cried Mavis.

2. Answers will vary.

page 124

```
d l a t e
r s t o p
y l o n g
b w e s t
o l e f t
y l o s e
```

a. stop

b. long

c. lose

d. dry

e. late

f. boy

g. west

h. left

page 125

1. *first column/synonym*

rock/stone

sick/ill

rug/mat

fast/quick

little/small

chair/seat

tidy/neat

2.

a. start

b. fix

c. nap

d. glad

page 126

1.

dog

table

train

flower

bus

book

street

cup

2.

a. lion

b. shop

c. salt

d. bed

e. chair

f. grass

page 127

1.

Sports–softball, football, golf, hockey

Colors–yellow, red, green, blue

Clothing–sweater, shoes, tie, socks

2.

a. drinks

b. colors

c. animals

d. flowers

e. vegetables

f. insects

page 128

1.

a. strawberry

b. teapot

c. notebook

d. windmill

e. starfish

f. bulldog

2.

a. lighthouse

b. toothbrush

c. popcorn

page 129

a. pan

b. rat

c. tap

d. arm

e. top

f. lips

page 130

1.

a. as busy as a bee

b. as slow as a snail

c. as light as a feather

d. as hot as fire

e. as wise as an owl

f. as cold as ice

2. Answers will vary.

a. as green as grass

b. as big as a giant

c. as flat as a rug

d. as strong as an ox

page 131

1.

a. ball

b. four

c. gate

d. boat

e. car

2.

a. one

b. arm

c. ear

d. lock

e. net

pages 132–135

Answers will vary.

page 136

1.

a. statement

b. question

c. question

d. exclamation

e. statement

2. Answers will vary.

3. Answers will vary.

page 137

Answers will vary.